D1524915

"All too often, history is driven by the mad passions and ambitions of tyrants—and by warped visions of "progress" crafted in the shadows behind their thrones. James Heiser's brilliant new book drags one of today's most dangerous "gray eminences" into the light. His careful, intricate analysis reveals Aleksandr Dugin, whose twisted ideology shapes Vladimir Putin's brutal and aggressive effort to build a Eurasian empire centered on Russia. This is a must-read for anyone who wants to understand the perilous and irrational motivations of those who now rule in Moscow."

—*Patrick Larkin, co-author of "Red Phoenix," "The Enemy Within," and other best-selling thrillers, and author of "The Tribune"*

"James Heiser has written a profoundly fascinating book on an important and troubling man. Anyone concerned about the future of Russia—indeed international affairs in general—should read this book."

—*Peter Schweizer, President, Government Accountability Institute, William J. Casey Fellow at the Hoover Institution, author, "Extortion," "Victory," and "Reagan's War"*

"A penetrating analysis of the dangerous totalitarian dogma of the man who has become Putin's Rasputin. If you want to understand the new threat to Western civilization, you need to read this book."

—*Dr. Robert Zubrin, President, Mars Society, President, Pioneer Astronautics and Pioneer Energy, author, "Merchants of Despair—Radical Environmentalists, Criminal Pseudo-Scientists, and the Fatal Cult of Antihumanism"*

"The American Empire Should Be Destroyed"

Aleksandr Dugin and the Perils of Immanentized Eschatology

"THE AMERICAN EMPIRE SHOULD BE DESTROYED"

Aleksandr Dugin and the Perils of Immanentized Eschatology

JAMES D. HEISER

REPRISTINATION PRESS
MALONE, TEXAS

REPRISTINATION PRESS
716 HCR 3424 E
MALONE, TEXAS 76660

www.repristinationpress.com

ISBN-13: 978-1891469435
ISBN-10: 1-891469-43-6

Table of Contents

Introduction: Ukraine, 31 March 2014

> *When there is only one power which decides who is*
> *right and who is wrong, and who should be punished and*
> *who not, we have a form of global dictatorship. This is not*
> *acceptable. Therefore, we should fight against it. If someone*
> *deprives us of our freedom, we have to react. And we will*
> *react. The American Empire should be destroyed. And at one*
> *point, it will be.*
>
> *...*
> *Spiritually, globalisation is the creation of a grand parody, the*
> *kingdom of the Antichrist. And the United States is the centre*
> *of its expansion.*[1]

Although the event received very little attention in the American media at the time, an arrest made by Ukrainian authorities in a park in the middle of Kiev may have exposed the machinations of a multinational movement which seeks to reshape the post-Cold War world. Oleg Bahtiyarov was arrested by Ukraine's security service (SBU) on March 31 on the charge that he was working to destabilize the country prior to the presidential elections scheduled for May 25:

> SBU stopped the illegal actions of O. Bahtiyarov who prepared a group of people under the guise of civil activists for the criminal seizure of the Ukrainian Verkhovna Rada and the Cabinet of Ministers of Ukraine.
>
> The offender attracted to his criminal intent up to 200 people, committing remuneration, organizing acquisition of "Molotov cocktails," bats, sliding ladders and other tools for storming government

1   Aleksandr Dugin, *The Fourth Political Theory,* trans. by Mark Sleboda and Michael Millerman (London: Arktos, 2012) p. 193.

buildings. O. Bahtiyarov promised participants in the assault monetary rewards up to $500 each. According to the plan, O. Bahtiyarov's assault was to destabilize Ukraine and disrupt the presidential election campaign. In addition to coverage of the assault on parliament and the cabinet, O. Bahtiyarov agreed with some Russian TV channels on filming the provocation.[2]

Bahtiyarov's involvement in the Ukrainian crisis as a purported *agent provocateur* might seem of little enduring interest if he were simply an agent of the Russian government; the world has long been accustomed to Soviet and Russian authorities conducting such operations both at home and abroad.[3] But Bahtiyarov's activities in Ukraine were extraordinary in several regards: first, because of the scope of his activities, and, second, because of his ideological affiliation. According to the SBU, Bahtiyarov's goal was to "forcibly take over government buildings ... planning to storm the country's parliament and Cabinet of Ministers buildings in Kyiv by force."[4] If true, such a provocative act on its own could have

2   "СБУ у центрі Києва затримала штурмовиків" (translated from the Ukrainian text) http://www.sbu.gov.ua/sbu/control/uk/publish/article?art_id=123171&cat_id=39574 [accessed 24 April 2014] Also see: "Alexander Dugin: The Crazy Ideologue of the New Russian Empire," www.thedailybeast.com/articles/2014/04/02/alexander-dugin-the-crazy-ideologue-of-the-new-russian-empire.html [accessed 19 April 2014]

3   See, for example, Richard H. Shultz and Roy Godson, *Dezinformatsia—The Strategy of Soviet Disinformation*, (New York: Berkley Books, 1986) p. 43–44.

4   Christopher J. Miller, "SBU detains Russian provacateur believed to have planned raid on parliament, cabinet buildings," www.kyivpost.com/content/ukraine/sbu-detains-russian-provacateur-believed-to-have-planned-raid-on-ukrainian-parliament-cabinet-341555.html [accessed 22 April 2014]

proven decisive in the outcome of the election, and given that Bahtiyarov allegedly had sufficient funds to organize a group of two hundred militants, it would seem that he might have been capable of implementing such a plan. But, even more chillingly, it is alleged that Bahtiyarov was not acting directly on behalf of the Russian government, but as an agent of an organization called the Eurasian Youth Union of Russia, the youth wing of the Eurasia Party established by Aleksandr Dugin. The actions of Bahtiyarov are thus of interest; the machinations of Aleksandr Dugin, the ideological father of Eurasianism, are of more enduring significance.

Dugin's position as an influential Russian academic who serves on the faculty of Moscow State University belies the full significance of the man both within the confines of Russia and within the greater context of modern Europe. As the chief modern proponent of the geopolitical doctrine known as "Eurasianism," Dugin has risen from the obscurity of the radical right and occult fringes of post-Soviet Russia to a place of influence in the innermost circles of Russian foreign policy. Although Dugin's doctrines are not well-known in the West, their effects are beginning to be seen.

The Ukrainian government has long recognized that Dugin is an enemy of Ukraine; in fact, the Ukrainian government formally declared him to be *persona non grata* for five years, beginning in June 2006, "for violating Ukrainian law".[5] When Dugin attempted to enter Ukraine in June 2007, the government deported him, "arguing he sought to destabilize the country." As a demonstration of Dugin's prominence within the Russian foreign policy apparatus, the Russian government retaliated within hours and refused to allow Mykola Zhulinsky to enter Russia. (Zhulinsky was then a senior aide

---

5   "Vitrenko's flirtation with Russian 'Neo-Eurasianism,'" www. kyivpost.com/opinion/op-ed/vitrenkos-flirtation-with-russian-neo-eurasianism-26787.html [accessed 22 April 2014]

12

to President Viktor Yushchenko.[6]) Dugin arguably proved the legitimacy of the Ukrainian action against him when, in 2009, he publicly advocated a Russian invasion of Ukraine.[7] The name of Aleksandr Dugin is one which is generally only recognized within certain academic circles; outside the ranks of those who are interested either in Russian foreign policy since the end of the 'Cold War' or who are students of particular esoteric strains of occultism, there has been little cause for the broader public to become aware of his existence. However, as the regime of Vladimir Vladimirovich Putin (1952–) has now begun to act on Dugin's geopolitical prognostications, the Eurasian ideology of Aleksandr Dugin—and the origins of that ideology—may no longer be ignored without peril to the West. A few years ago, scholars could shake their heads in disbelief at Dugin's eclectic—even bizarre—mix of sources; for example, Wayne Allensworth wrote of Dugin's "fascination with the occult (including Satanism)" and wrote of the "postmodern quality of Dugin's eclectic philosophy, including European geopolitics and strategy, Gnostic mysticism, occultism, 'traditionalism,' and his advocacy of 'leftist fascism and rightist communism.'"[8] As early as 1993, Walter

6   "Ukraine slams Russia for barring president's top aide from entry," www.kyivpost.com/content/business/ukraine-slams-russia-for-barring-presidents-top-ai-26724.html [accessed 22 April 2014]

7   "United Press International reports that Alexander Dugin, a Russian expansionist at Moscow State University, thinks the gas war shows the Kremlin need [sic] to go on the offensive. Russia may need to 'split Ukraine, establish protectorate over the eastern and southern parts and then introduce a different political leadership there. On the whole, we should attack; otherwise we will have to give up, both in gas and other spheres.'" "Russian analyst rattles sabers over gas" (2 February 2009), www.kyivpost.com/content/world/russian-analyst-rattles-sabers-over-gas-34704.html [accessed 22 April 2014]

8   Wayne Allensworth, "Dugin and the Eurasian controversy" in *Russian Nationalism and the National Reassertion of Russia,* ed. by Marlène Laruelle (London and New York: Routledge, 2009) p. 116.

Laqueur observed that "With Dugin we move from the realm of a quasi-rational approach to the depths of irrationality. ... For Dugin, the inventor of 'conspiratology,' world history has to be rewritten. The eternal conflict between Atlanticists and Eurasians began in ancient Egypt and it leads to the struggle between the good (Eurasian) and bad (Atlanticist)."[9]

Today, it is no longer safe to ignore the ideology of Aleksandr Dugin. No matter how "irrational," Dugin's ideology now influences the foreign policy of one of the most significant regional powers in the modern world. When a man whose worldview is allegedly shaped by a "fascination with the occult" proclaims that "the American Empire must be destroyed" because it is at the center of the expansion of the "kingdom of the Antichrist," the real universe has been left behind in exchange for a 'counterverse'—a gnosticized realm of 'conspiratology' and that which Eric Voegelin referred to as "immanentized eschatology": the moment when groups of men possessed by a gnostic ideology attempt to remake the world to conform to their fantasies.

---

9   Walter Laqueur, *Black Hundred—The Rise of the Extreme Right in Russia* (New York: HarperCollins, 1993) p. 266.

Prisci Theologi and Traditionalism

> *I share the vision of René Guénon and Julius Evola, who considered modernity and its ideological basis (individualism, liberal democracy, capitalism, consumerism, and so on) to be the cause of the future catastrophe of humanity, and the global domination of the Western lifestyle as the reason for the final degradation of the Earth.*[10]

To properly understand the worldview of Aleksandr Dugin, it is necessary to understand him in the context of an intellectual movement which purports to be as old as the Modern era—a movement which is now known as "Traditionalism." It is not that "Traditionalism" *per se* enjoys such an ancient pedigree—the current movement which calls itself by this name only dates to the 1920s and 1930s—but the Traditionalists present themselves as the latest iteration of a religious movement which can be traced to the earliest days of the Italian Renaissance. This claim by the Traditionalists is problematic in certain key regards and it certainly does not give proper credit to many of the accomplishments of the scholars of the Renaissance. But the existence of modern Traditionalism is connected to an aspect of the heritage of the Renaissance by means of the "law of unintended consequences."

In his history of the modern "Traditionalist" movement, Mark Sedgwick observes: "The term *philosophia perennis* (Perennial Philosophy) was coined in 1540 by a Catholic scholar to describe one of the central insights of Marsilio Ficino, an important figure in the origins of Traditionalism."[11]

10   Dugin, *The Fourth Political Theory*, p. 193.
11   Mark Sedgwick, *Against the Modern World—Traditionalism and the Secret Intellectual History of the Twentieth Century*, (Oxford, New York: Oxford University Press, 2004) p. 23.

16

Sedgwick's identification of Ficino (1433–1499) as an "important figure" is certainly correct; in fact, the influence of Ficino's promotion of the *prisci theologi*—the "ancient theologians" of pagan antiquity—had a profoundly significant influence on the course of the Renaissance. Ficino's role as the ideological ancestor of "Traditionalism" (also called "Perennialism") was of significance for the course of "Traditionalism" in his era and in our present generation:

> For a century and a half after Ficino, the idea that there was a Perennial Philosophy became increasingly widely accepted. Perennialism was, however, discredited in the early seventeenth century and thereafter survived only at the edges of Western intellectual life. Then, in the nineteenth century, Perennialism was revived in a slightly modified form, with the newly discovered Vedas being taken as its surviving textual form.[12]

Given the historical parallels between the origins and course of Renaissance-era Traditionalism and the modern variety, we ask the reader's indulgence of a brief recapitulation of that earlier history.

In *Prisci Theologi and the Hermetic Reformation in the Fifteenth Century*,[13] the present author offered an account of the origins of aspects of Ficino's thought in the philosophical-theological writings attributed to a mythic figure of antiquity known as "Hermes Trismegistus" (Thrice-Great Hermes). In the Middle Ages and Renaissance, Hermes Trismegistus was widely believed to have been a pagan contemporary of Moses. From the perspective of Western Christendom, the one extant work attributed to Hermes—the *Asclepius*—was known to the ancient Christian fathers, and had earned the disap-

---

12   Sedgwick, p. 24.
13   (Malone, Texas: Repristination Press, 2011).

probation of St. Augustine, who condemned Hermes for his promotion of an "impious art" of summoning demons into statues. Apart from the *Asclepius,* the name of Hermes was associated with the art of alchemy. Thus, before the age of Ficino, Hermes had almost ceased to have a direct impact on European thought.

The reassessment of Hermes Trismegistus came about because of the influence that Gemistos Plethon—a representative of Eastern Orthodoxy at the Council of Ferrara-Florence (1438–1455)—had upon Cosimo de'Medici (1389–1464), who was the founder of the Medici dynasty in Florence. The intersection of Gemistos Plethon and Cosimo de'Medici had a profound impact on the history of the West because during his time in Florence in 1438 and 1439, Gemistos inspired Cosimo to establish a Platonic Academy. Gemistos brought the doctrines and Cosimo provided the monetary support which established the Hermetic Reformation—a 'reform' of Church teaching based on Hermetic doctrines—in Florence through the translation and literary efforts of Marsilio Ficino, whom Cosimo personally selected for the task of establishing the academy and translating newly-discovered writings of Hermes Trismegistus.

Gemistos was vehemently opposed to any reunification between the churches of the West and East which had been divided since the "Great Schism" of 1053. However, it would seem doubtful that his vehemence was rooted in the doctrine of Eastern Orthodoxy, because Plethon was secretly a neo-pagan—a fact attested by his fellow adherents of Eastern Orthodoxy who were present for the council. As George Trapezuntius related in 1455: "I myself heard him [Gemistos] at Florence—for he came to the Council with the Greeks—asserting that the whole world would in a few years adopt one and the same religion, with one mind, one intelligence, one teaching. And when I asked: 'Christ's or Muhammad's?' he replied: 'Neither, but one not differing from paganism.'"[14] The accuracy of this assessment is upheld by modern scholars who have studied Gemistos' teachings:

> ... Gemistos, who had no idea of the comparative antiquity of religions, looked at Zoroaster, Moses, and various legendary Greeks as the nominal sources of his system. But he formulated its content in terms of what he believed to be the oldest surviving religion, and also the best known to him, which was the Olympian religion of his ancestors, including its pre-Olympian core. This reversion to paganism on his part was deliberatively provocative, but it was not mere foolishness.[15]

Gemistos Plethon believed that there was a pagan equivalent of an 'apostolic succession' of doctrine and this sense of a succession of divinely-inspired pagan teachers would be carried over into the work of Marsilio Ficino.[16] Beginning with Ficino, a fundamental tenet of what would later become "Traditionalism" entered Western thought: that different religions were divinely-inspired, with various 'heathen' nations receiving their own salvific revelations from God. Ficino sought to fundamentally alter the Christian concept of the relationship between Christian doctrine and other religions:

> There were two main theories that allowed the adoption of these doctrines [the teachings of the *prisci theologi*] into a Christian monotheistic framework: the first contends that they agree with Christian theology because they were influenced by a primeval tradition which included or at least adumbrated the tenets of

---

14   quoted in C.M. Woodhouse, *Gemistos Plethon—The Last of the Hellenes,* (Oxford: Clarendon Press, 2000), p. 168.
15   ibid., p. 169.
16   see Heiser, *Prisci Theologi and the Hermetic Reformation in the Fifteenth Century,* p. 35–46.

Christianity; the alternative argues that the affinity between these two bodies of thought has no historical explanation but is a result of a revelation or a series of revelations imparted separately to both pagan and monotheistic spiritual leaders.[17]

As noted previously, the pivotal moment in the Hermetic Reformation came when Ficino translated the *Corpus Hermeticum*—a collection of writings attributed to Hermes Trismegistus which were brought to Florence in 1460. Cosimo de'Medici placed such a high priority on the translation of the *Corpus* that he immediately set Ficino to work on them. In the memorable assessment of Frances Yates:

> Though the Plato manuscripts were already assembled, awaiting translation, Cosimo ordered Ficino to put these aside and to translate the work of Hermes Trismegistus at once, before embarking on the Greek philosophers. ... But in the year 1463 word came to Ficino from Cosimo that he must translate Hermes first, at once, and then go on afterwards to Plato; ... Ficino made the translation in a few months, whilst the old Cosimo, who died in 1464, was still alive. Then he began on Plato.
>
> It was an extraordinary situation. There are the complete works of Plato, waiting, and they must wait whilst Ficino quickly translates Hermes, probably because Cosimo wants to read him before he dies. What a testimony this is to the mysterious reputation of the Thrice Great One![18]

17   Moshe Idel, "Prisca Theologia in Marsilio Ficino," in *Marsilio Ficino: His Theology, His Philosophy, His Legacy,* ed. by Michael J. B. Allen and Valery Rees with Martin Davies, (Leiden, Boston, Köln: Brill, 2002), p. 138–9.

18   Frances A. Yates, *Giordano Bruno and the Hermetic Tradition,* (Chicago: The University of Chicago Press, 1964) p. 12–13.

Ficino's syncretistic doctrine established a context in which he and his followers could borrow from other "Traditions"—beginning with Neoplatonism and Jewish Kabbalah—seeking a commonality of revelation between the various religions. It is hardly surprising that adherents of other religions are often infuriated by such attempts to co-opt their beliefs in service of another religion; syncretism also undermines the faith of those who attempt to so misuse the sacred writings of other religions. (Thus, for example, when Ficino wrote the eighteen volumes of his *Platonic Theology*, he presented a false view of both Christian *and* Neoplatonic teachings.[19]) The efforts by Ficino and like-minded Renaissance era syncretists ultimately failed when those "ancient theologians" proved not to have been so ancient, after all.[20] And, in fact, efforts to syncretize the teachings of two religions never brings unity—it simply creates a *third* religion. This was the fate of the Hermetic Reformation of Ficino, and it is the fate of its ideological descendant, Traditionalism, in the twentieth century. We have offered this brief recapitulation of the roots of Traditionalism to serve as a lesson for the present: **Traditionalism offers a fictionalized account of the prehistoric past as a means of imposing a fictionalized view of the course of history on the present.** An attendant consequence of this lesson is that when Traditionalism is exposed as a fiction, it damages the reputation of those who were beguiled by its doctrines—a taint which adheres to Ficino's reputation to this day.

19   See Heiser, *Prisci Theologi*, p. 65–198.

20   For example, the *Corpus Hermeticum* proved not to be as ancient as Ficino (and others) imagined: rather than being contemporary with the earliest books of the Old Testament, the *Corpus* was clearly composed well into the Christian era. Thus the points of similarity between Christianity and Hermeticism which Ficino and others trumpeted in the texts were not a 'separate revelation,' but a Gnostic borrowing from Christian sources.

Scholars such as Marsilio Ficino never would have imagined (and certainly never intended) that their labors would be utilized by a movement such as Traditionalism or by a man such as Aleksandr Dugin. But, in his naïveté, Ficino (and other scholars) unleashed syncretic notions which the fathers of Traditionalism exploited. Thus the legacy of some Renaissance scholars is that their religious syncretism is exploited by movements as diverse as "New Age" occultism and Traditionalism. What began as a quest for understanding is now exploited in an effort to obscure the truth.

The history of modern Traditionalism is complicated by a vast array of characters and subtle distinctions of doctrine which are often almost incomprehensible to those who are not adherents of its dogmas. For purposes of brevity, we cite Sedgwick's summary of the twentieth century movement:

> The history of Traditionalism falls into three stages... During the first stage, up to the 1930s, [René] Guénon developed the Traditionalist philosophy, wrote various articles and books, and gathered a small group of followers. During the second stage, attempts were made to put the Traditionalist philosophy into practice, principally in two very different contexts: Sufi Islam, as an example of Oriental metaphysics, and European fascism, as a form of revolt. During the third stage, after the 1960s, Traditionalist ideas began to merge unremarked into the general culture of the West and to pass from the West to the Islamic world and to Russia.[21]

For purposes of examining the influence of Traditionalism on Aleksandr Dugin, two figures repeatedly appear in his writings: René Guénon (1886–1951) and Julius Evola (1898–1974). While Guénon is the defining figure of the first period of Traditionalist history, the division between Guénon and Evola

21   Sedgwick, p. 22.

defines the period which Sedgwick sets forth as the second phase of the history of the movement. In Sedgwick's words:

> For Guénon, the transformation of the individual through initiation was the means for the transformation of the West as a whole through the influence of the elite. ... To judge from Evola's own actions, however, the transformation of the individual was to be not so much the means as the *consequence* of the transformation of society. Although even at the end of his life Evola was uncertain about the means to *individual* self-realization, his views on the transformation of society seem to have been definite from the start.[22]

For Guénon, his rejection of the course of Western civilization and his attempts to restore that civilization led to the personal action of converting to Islam. For Evola, a bitter rejection of "bourgeois Christian values" led him first to embrace Friedrich Neitzsche's doctrine of the *Übermensch* (superman) and later to join Guénon's rejection of modern Western civilization in favor of Traditionalism, albeit by means of advocating authoritarianism as the cultural reform. However, for both 'branches' of Traditionalism, there is a common rejection of the Modern age. In the words of one Traditionalist scholar:

> For the traditionalists modernism is nothing less than a spiritual disease which continues to spread like a plague across the globe, decimating traditional cultures wherever they are still to be found. Although its historical origins are European, modernism is now tied to no specific area or civilization. ... Scientism, rationalism, relativism, materialism, positivism, empiricism, psychologism, individualism, humanism, existentialism: these are some of the prime follies of

22   ibid., p. 100–101.

modernist thought. ... Behind the somewhat bizarre array of ideologies which have proliferated in the last few centuries the traditionalists discern a growing and persistent ignorance concerning the ultimate realities and an indifference, if not always an overt hostility, to the eternal verities conveyed by tradition.[23]

In place of the "–isms" of the modern age, the Traditionalists seek for the restoration of the influences of the "Primordial Tradition":

This timeless wisdom has carried many names: *philosophia perennis, Lex Aeterna, Hagia Sophia, Din al-Haqq, Akālika Dhamma* and *Sanātana Dharma* are among the better known. ... This universal wisdom, in existence since the dawn of time and the spiritual patrimony of all humankind, can also be designated as the Primordial Tradition.[24]

Given Guénon's and Evola's rejection of Christianity, the writings of Traditionalists can often leave the Christian reader with the sense that all 'traditions' convey such "Primordial Tradition"—*except* Western Christianity.[25] Evola has proven to be the particular favorite among adherents of Traditionalism who are opposed to Christianity; thus, as Stéphane François recently observed regarding the French *Nouvelle Droite* (New Right): "Evola has greatly influenced sectors of the ND who wish to degrade or destroy two thousand years of Christianity's heritage in Europe."[26] Because Evola's emphasis was

23   Kenneth Oldmeadow, *Traditionalism—Religion in the light of Perennial Philosophy,* (Colombo: The Sri Lanka Institute of Traditional Studies, 2000) p. 117.
24   ibid., p. 59.
25   Even Oldmeadow refers to "certain vulnerabilities in Christian civilization" (p. 117) as the source of the evils of modernity.
26   Stéphane François, "The *Nouvelle Droite* and 'Tradition,'" in

24

on the restoration of the individual by means of transformation of society, his "first known activity on becoming a Traditionalist was to attempt to guide Fascist society toward
Traditionalism."[27] Evola's linkage of Traditionalism and authoritarianism continues to exert an influence on his followers to this day:

> It is important to stress that, aside from Tradi-
> tionalism, the ND [Nouvelle Droite] often incorporates
> other currents of radical right-wing thought: Europe-
> an nationalism, anti-Semitism disguised as anti-Zion-
> ism, Nazi occultism, Nordic traditions, ethnocentrism,
> and the extreme right-wing, neo-fascist milieu, etc. It
> is no accident, then, that both Evola and sectors of the
> Traditionalist ND have praised the Legion of the Arch-
> angel Michael, its paramilitary unit the Iron Guard
> formed in 1930, and its Romanian fascist leader Cor-
> neliu Codreanu. The Iron Guard "legionnaires" were
> partly influenced by Traditionalism, particularly their
> attachment to Orthodox Christianity and Romania's
> popular folk traditions.[28]

It is not surprising, therefore, given his attachment to the
teachings of Evola, that Aleksandr Dugin's first political involvement was with the extremist *Pamyat'* movement, attempting to inculcate Traditionalism in its ranks (an effort
which will be discussed in the next chapter).

Misunderstandings of Dugin's Traditionalism

As noted at the beginning of the chapter, and as Dugin
himself has asserted through his multitudinous writings on
the topic of Traditionalism, the Traditionalism of Guénon and

27   Sedgwick, p. 101.
28   François, p. 96.

Evola (with a marked preference for the latter teacher) is the very cornerstone of his worldview. In her study of Dugin's teaching, Laruelle describes Traditionalism as the "foundation" of Dugin's thought and observes:

> The influence of Traditionalism on Dugin seems to be fundamental: it constitutes his main intellectual reference point and the basis of his political attitudes as well as his Eurasianism. Dugin has made considerable efforts to disseminate Traditionalist thought in Russia. He regularly translates extracts from the works of the great Traditionalist theoreticians, René Guénon and Julius Evola, but also from so-called "soft" Traditionalist authors such as Mircea Eliade and Carl Jung; so-called "hard" Traditionalists like Titus Burckhardt; converts to Sufism, such as Frithjof Schuon; and converts to Islamism, like Claudio Mutti. The journals *Elementy*, and, especially, *Milyi angel*, whose full subtitle is "Metaphysics, angelology, cosmic cycles, eschatology, and tradition," are dedicated to the diffusion of Traditionalist thought.[29]

In fact, it was Dugin's status as a Traditionalist which first called him to the attention of the present author while he was engaged in a study of the ongoing influence of Ficino's *prisci theologi*. However, given the fringe character of the Traditionalist movement, and the propensity of its adherents to become involved in occultism and extremist politics, many mainstream scholars are not equipped to fully understand the character of Traditionalist thought. Unless one understands that Dugin's Traditionalism provides a fundamentally theological character to his cultural and geopolitical procla-

---

29   Marlene Laruelle, *Aleksandr Dugin: A Russian Version of the European Radical Right?*, (Washington, D.C.: Kennan Institute, 2006) Occasional Paper #294. p. 10.

26

mations and prognostications, it is impossible to grasp the heart of his position.

One example of such a failure to understand Traditionalism is seen in Edith Clowes' *Russia on the Edge—Imagined Geographies and Post Soviet Identity*. Clowes devotes a chapter to Dugin and in many regards has a clear understanding of the danger posed by his views, seeing in his ideology "an idea of Russianness that combines a strange mix of Slavophile values, Eurasianist thought from the 1920s, neofascism, and, finally, a wildly different orientation toward what he calls postmodernism."[30] However, as will be explored in greater depth later, Dugin's "Eurasianism" is markedly different from the Eurasianism of the 1920s, because it has been fundamentally reshaped by his Traditionalism. Because Clowes apparently does not understand the universalistic religious propensities of Traditionalism, she fails to understand the way in which Dugin expresses a toleration for other religions, and apparently believes that Dugin's 'toleration' is only hypocrisy:

> Along with political hypocrisy comes religious hypocrisy. Dugin combines a desire to seem tolerant of all ethnic groups and religions, particularly ancient ones, with an affirmation of the superiority of Russian Orthodoxy as the state religion. In Eurasia there are several dominant religions—Christianity, Islam, Buddhism, Judaism, Taoism, as well as "archaic cults." Eurasianism, Dugin claims, welcomes ethnic and religious differences ... while at the same time asserting the "universal mission of the Orthodox Church"[31]

---

30   Edith Clowes, *Russia on the Edge—Imagined Geographies and Post-Soviet Identity*, (Ithaca and London: Cornell University Press, 2011) p. 44.
31   ibid., p. 63.

However, this is precisely the character of Dugin's religious views as a Traditionalist. As Andreas Umland observed in 2007: "... as a result of the impact of integral Traditionalism for Dugin's thought, he has distanced himself from the classical Eurasianist view of Orthodoxy as being superior to Islam."[32] Again, in Umland's words:

> While the classical Eurasianists had also sympathies for Islam, they wrote negatively about the Koran. They attacked Eastern religions—not the least Buddhism—as being "Satanic." Dugin, on the contrary, has openly shown sympathy for many Eastern religions, and made positive references to representatives of Western Satanism. For Dugin, Orthodoxy by itself plays obviously a less important role than it did for the classical Eurasianists who were already by their upbringing devout Orthodox believers. Dugin, in contrast, has only recently become a member of an Orthodox Church of the Old Belief which, however, accepts the supremacy of the Moscow Patriarchy. **Being framed by the ideas of Evola and other Traditionalists, Dugin sees Orthodoxy only as one of several religions that have preserved the initial "Tradition." No such ideas can be found in classical Eurasianism.**[33] [emphasis added]

While Dugin appears to be committed to the Old Believer sect among the Russian Orthodox, he is far from being a 'fundamentalist'; in fact, he has publicly expressed a disinterest in linking actual participation in the liturgical life of the Church with adherence to the Orthodox faith. In Dugin's words: "I

---

32   Andreas Umland, "Post-Soviet 'Uncivil Society' and the Rise of Aleksandr Dugin—A Case Study in Extraparliamentary Radical Right in Contemporary Russia (Ph.D. dissertation, Trinity College-Cambridge, 2007) p. 150.

33   ibid., p. 151.

28

do not support a strict division of Orthodox Christians into church-goers and non-goers. I think that everyone who identifies himself with Orthodoxy is Orthodox."[34] Such an indifference to participation in the rites of the Church seems utterly incongruous with membership in a sacramental, liturgical, and hierarchical church such as the Russian Orthodox Church. But Dugin's affirmation of Russian Orthodoxy actually reduces the Church to a cultural artifact and a civil institution. As Anastasia Mitrofanova observed in her groundbreaking study of the politicization of Orthodoxy in Russia:

> Orthodoxy is increasingly perceived as a kind of civil religion: all citizens of Russia are automatically considered "Orthodox," except for members of several legally recognized confessions who are seen as "the Orthodox *honoris causa.*" ...

> The idea of a union between the traditional religions of Russia, in which Orthodoxy is the leading component of an emerging civil religion, appears to have been borrowed from the doctrine of Eurasianism. Indeed, this influence seems natural since Eurasianist ideology permits the integration of different ethnic groups and confessions into a single nation.[35]

Thus, Dugin's syncretic "toleration" is not hypocrisy; rather, it is Traditionalism in action, which, in turn, threatens Russian Orthodoxy with a vitiation of meaning in exchange for universality.

It appears that Clowes fundamentally fails to understand the mystical aspect of Dugin's "sacred geography." While this misunderstanding is hardly surprising (after all, the tenets of sacred geography are even more historically

---

34   Quoted in Anastasia Mitrofanova, *The Politicization of Russian Orthodoxy—Actors and Ideas,* (Stuttgart: Ibidem-Verlag, 2005) p. 137.
35   ibid., p. 177.

remote from the Modern mind than those of alchemy), nevertheless it leads to a mistaken notion of what Dugin means when he speaks in terms of "Northern"—even "nordic"—civilization. In Clowes' words:

> The key factor in Dugin's thinking about identity is geographical space. In this point he follows the lead of Nazi geopolitical thinkers, the Eurasianists, and the Soviet-era ethnologist Gumilev, who theorized that identity and mentality are determined by geographical and meteorological environment. ... His first concern is to establish the north's—and especially Moscow's—significance as "sacred ground," extending from prehistoric pagan times to the post-Soviet present, as the political, economic, and cultural center of all Eurasia.[36]

Again, this claim rests on a fundamental misunderstanding of Dugin's mystical mindset. In the essay, "From Sacred Geography to Geopolitics,"[37] Dugin makes at clear that the origins of his understanding of geopolitics is radically removed from those who view that field in terms of modern science; in fact, he likens the roots of geopolitics to alchemy and magic:

> Geopolitics in its present form is undoubtedly a worldly, "profane", secularized science. But maybe, among all modern sciences, it saved in itself the greatest connection with Tradition and traditional sciences. René Guénon said that modern chemistry is the outcome of the desacralization of a traditional science—alchemy, as modern physics is of magic. Exactly in the same way one might say that modern geopolitics is the product of the laicizing and desacralizing of another traditional science—sacred geography. ... The connec-

---

36   Clowes, p. 55.
37   available online: http://evrazia.info/article/416 [Accessed May 19, 2014]

tion with sacred geography here is rather distinctly visible. Therefore it is possible to say that geopolitics stands in an intermediate place between traditional science (sacred geography) and profane science.

Thus, when Dugin imposes the notions of his Traditionalist account of sacred geography (a geography which is drawn from the writings of Guénon and Evola), his delineation of the spiritual characteristics of "North," "South," "East" and "West" are carefully decoupled from crass racism. Thus, for example, Dugin wrote of the spiritual virtues of the "North": "The most ancient and original layer of Tradition univocally affirms the primacy of the North above the South. The symbolism of North relates to a Source, to an original northern paradise, from where all human civilization originates." Taken in isolation, such a quotation might cause one to imagine that Dugin's views of the "North" track with the racial notions of the National Socialists. However, Dugin takes the symbolic significance of "North" in a very different direction:

Therefore it is possible to say that all sacred traditions are in essence the projection of a Single Northern Primordial Tradition adapted to every different historical condition. North is Cardinal Point chosen by the primeval Logos in order to reveal itself in History, and each of its further manifestations only restored that primeval polar-paradise symbolism. ...

Thus it is important to mark that in sacred geography the North-South axis is more relevant than the East-West axis. But being the more relevant one, it corresponds to the most ancient stages of cyclical history. The great war of North and South, Hyperborea and Gondvana (ancient paleo-continent of the South) refers to "antidiluvian" [sic] times. In the last phases of the cycle it becomes more hidden, veiled. The paleo-continents of North and South themselves disappear. The testimonial sign of opposition is passed to East and West.

For Dugin, this means that a civilization being of the "North"—even "nordic"—has nothing to do with worldly geography or skin color; rather, it is a spiritual disposition:

> The pure nordic civilization disappeared with the ancient Hyperboreans, but its messengers have laid the bases of all present traditions. This nordic "race" of Teachers stood at the origins of religion and culture of the peoples of all continents and colours of skin. Traces of an hyperborean cult can be found among the Indians of Northern America and among the ancient Slaves [sic], among the founders of the Chinese civilization and among the natives of the Pacific, among the blond Germans and among the black shamans of Western Africa, among the red-skinned Aztecs and among the Mongols with wide cheek-bones. ... True spirituality, suprarational Mind, divine Logos, capacity to see through the world its secret Soul—these are the defining qualities of the North. Wherever there is Sacred Purity and Wisdom, there invisibly is the North—whatever the point in time or space we are in.

People who speak of Hyperborea as a historical place are eccentric, at best, but Dugin has actually steered such talk away from the more crass, racist notions which have been linked with geographical, racial determinism in the past. As we will see later, Dugin's notion of the men of 'Arctogaia'/Hyperborea is such that they are spread everywhere, as a spiritual elite which is perpetually at war with the mundane, materialist men of the "South"—wherever they may live throughout the nations and 'races' of mankind.

32

Again, Clowes objects that Dugin "affirms subjective mythical thinking, while callously dismissing personal feelings, experiences and relationships, and private rights."[38] But for Dugin, mythical thinking is entirely in keeping with Traditionalist thought, and would be perceived to be far from "subjective"; actually, the Traditionalist would see the myth as the "real" thing, while "feelings, experiences, relationships, rights" are all inherently individual, and thus subjective, and—Dugin would likely argue—artifacts of modernism. Clowes complains that "In his imagined world we encounter the anti-modern, anti-scientific, conservative-utopian views that mark fascist thought."[39] The source of Dugin's views is in Traditionalism's opposition to the Modern age: like Evola before him, Dugin is led to authoritarian political views by his Traditionalist dogmas, not vice versa.

A different misunderstanding is found in an essay by Andreas Umland, who has otherwise proven an insightful critic of Dugin's thought. In his 2009 article for *The Russian Review* ("Is Aleksandr Dugin a Traditionalist? 'Neo-Eurasianism and Perennial Philosophy'")[40], Umland endeavors to deprive Dugin of any standing as a legitimate representative of Traditionalism—and of Eurasianism, for that matter. Umland's line of attack is an attempt to deprive Evola of his standing as a Traditionalist thinker and thus, since Dugin's Traditionalism is primarily witnessed in his adherence to Evola's thought, exclude Dugin from the ranks of 'true' Traditionalists. While there is little doubt that there are many disciples of 'pure' Guénonian Traditionalism who would like to expel Evola and his disciples from the circles of the 'faithful,' this is a rather familiar occurrence within religious groups.

One cannot avoid a simple truth enunciated by Sedg-

38   Clowes, p. 47.
39   ibid.
40   *The Russian Review* 68 (October 2009): 662–78.

wick: "Evola's name later came to be linked by many with Guénon's own as a co-founder of Traditionalism, and Evola was arguably Guénon's most important collaborator".[41] It is true that Guénon emphasized the individual transformation, while Evola sought first the transformation of society, but this does not eliminate their common affirmation of a Primordial Tradition which stands in an enduring opposition to a Modernism which threatens civilization (to speak in Traditionalist terms). While Umland might seek to 'excommunicate' Dugin from the ranks of the Traditionalist 'faithful' by first removing Evola in like fashion, the history of the Traditionalist movement will not admit such a revision at this late date. Whatever else one may say regarding Alexandr Dugin, one must concede that he is a Traditionalist of very fixed convictions, and he is prepared to remake the world in keeping with that Traditionalist doctrine.

It is also of no small concern to take into consideration the way in which Dugin describes the relationship of his own ideological views to those of Traditionalism. Umland observes that Dugin describes Traditionalism as *the* major influence on his worldview; Dugin declared in a 2006 interview:

> [My] intellectual formation happened in 1979–1980 when becoming acquainted with the traditionalists of the "third way," those like [Eduard] Golovin and [Geidar] Dzhemal. Therefore my formation as a personality, as an intellectual, as a thinker, as a politician, as an ideologue was exactly traditionalistic. [...] I was 17–18 years old and saw the world as absolutely empty and disgusting. This emptiness had to be filled with something. The alternatives which were offered to me—the intelligentsia with [Bulat] Okudzhava, half-dissidents reading [Aleksandr] Solzhenitsyn, the inert conformist Orthodox—did not fill this emptiness

41   Sedgwick, p. 98.

at all [...]. The only thing which could fill this gigantic inner emptiness which I had was the total rejection of everything modern within the framework of the ultra-revolutionary non-conformist intellectualism of [René] Guénon and [Julius] Evola. [...] That is how I was formed. In 1981–82, I was already a full-fledged [*zakonchennyi*] philosopher with my own intellectual agenda, with an own [sic] metaphysic and ideology. [...] I did not mature any more [*Bol'she ya ne vzroslel*].[42]

Not surprisingly, Laruelle observed in the same year (2006): "[Dugin] continues even today to disseminate the Traditionalist ideas that have been his mainstay since the beginning, displaying a high degree of doctrinal consistency."[43]

42   quoted in Andreas Umland, "Post-Soviet 'Uncivil Society' and the Rise of Aleksandr Dugin—A Case Study in Extraparliamentary Radical Right in Contemporary Russia (Ph.D. dissertation, Trinity College-Cambridge, 2007) p. 147.

43   Laruelle, *Aleksandr Dugin: A Russian Version of the European Radical Right?*, p. 5.

An Overview of the Life of Aleksandr Dugin

"Chaos can think."[44]

For most of his life and intellectual career, Aleksandr Ge-
lyevich Dugin (1962–) seemed an unlikely prospect for
achieving prominence in Russian society. In 1993, Laqueur
declared near the conclusion of his assessment of extremist
organizations in post-Soviet Russia:

> Some Moscow intellectuals have been borrowing
> heavily from the postfascist *Nouvelle Droite*. But it is
> most unlikely that the rehash of geopolitics and Eur-
> asianism, of Judeo-Masonic conspiracy theories re-
> cycled as "mondialism," and of German metaphysical
> philosophy with an admixture of neopaganism will
> ever amount to more than the parlor games of a hand-
> ful of intellectuals.[45]

It appears to be Laqueur's intention to give a precise summa-
tion of Dugin's ideological matrix and then to dismiss that
matrix as little more than the basis for "parlor games." It is
difficult to criticize Laqueur's assessment, apart from the
benefits of hindsight. In the West, where views such as those
upheld by Dugin are the domain of the French "New Right"
(*Nouvelle Droite*)—typified, for example, by the writings of
Alain de Benoist (e.g., *On Being a Pagan*)—and the American
theatrum absurdum provided by a bevy of racist neopagan
organizations,[46] the notion that the core beliefs of what con-

44   Alexander Dugin, *The Fourth Political Theory,* trans. by Mark
Sleboda and Michael Millerman (London: Arktos,2012) p. 210.
45   Walter Laqueur, *Black Hundred—The Rise of the Extreme
Right in Russia* (New York: HarperCollins, 1993) p. 291.
46   For a recent history of racist neopaganism see Mattias Gardell,

36

stitutes the "lunatic fringe" in one country could become the political center in another country is difficult to accept. However, the emergence of Eurasianism as an "armed doctrine" signals quite clearly that the time in which one could hope simply to ignore Dugin is now past. When it comes to understanding the seemingly-complicated strands which come together in Dugin's thought, it is important to realize that the various sources of his ideology do not reflect a development in his position; that is, it is not that he started from the standpoint of an occultist and later developed into a philosopher. Instead, as Marlene Laruelle notes:

> Several intellectual tendencies manifest themselves in his thought: a political theory inspired by Traditionalism, Orthodox religious philosophy, Aryanist and occultist theories, and geopolitical and Eurasianist conceptions. One might expect this ideological diversity to reflect a lengthy evolution in Dugin's intellectual life. Quite to the contrary, however, all these topics did not emerge in succession but have co-existed in Dugin's writings since the beginning of the 1990s.[47]

Dugin was born into a family which was distinguished for its military service; in the words of one scholar, "Dugin grew up in a privileged family as the son of a *GRU* (the Soviet military intelligence agency) officer, either a general or a colonel, and that his grand-father and great-grandfather had

Gods of the Blood—The Pagan Revival and White Separatism, (Durham and London: Duke University Press, 2003) and Nicholas Goodrick-Clarke, *Black Sun—Aryan Cults, Esoteric Nazism and the Politics of Identity,* (New York and London: New York University Press, 2002).
47   Marlene Laruelle, *Aleksandr Dugin: A Russian Version of the European Radical Right?,* (Washington, D.C.: Kennan Institute, 2006) p. 1. Occasional Paper #294.

also been army officers."⁴⁸ The service which Dugin would render to his country is arguably quite different from that of his ancestors, but it is nonetheless one which is oriented toward warfare.

The Yuzhinskii Circle

Very little has been published to date in the West regarding Dugin's formative years that does not center on his fixation with the occult, for it appears that he turned to the occult at an early phase of life. Shenfield presents the young Aleksandr Dugin in terms which many readers might see as indicative of a easy 'mark' for a cult: "Depressed and alienated from the Soviet reality around him, he encountered by chance, through a neighbor of his parents, a secretive group of intellectuals who gave him the existential home he sought."⁴⁹ Thus, by 1980, he had joined the 'circle' of Yevgeny Golovin—a group which is known as the "Yuzhinskii circle," taking its name from the street upon which its founder—Yuri Mamleyev (Mamleev)—resided. Umland briefly recounts the involvement of Mamleyev and Golovin prior to Dugin's entrance into the "circle":

> Most sources agree that the Yuzhinskii circle had been founded in the 1960s at the flat of Yurii Mamleev (b. 1931), a well-known Russian mysticist, novelist and metaphysic. ... Having been forced to emigrate in 1975, Mamleev went first to the United States where he taught at Cornell University and, in 1983, to France where he taught at the Sorbonne. In 1991, he returned

48   Andreas Umland, "Aleksandr Dugin's transformation from a lunatic fringe figure into a mainstream political publicist, 1980–1998: A case study in the rise of late and post-Soviet Russian fascism," *Journal of Eurasian Studies* 1 (2010). p. 145.
49   Stephen D. Shenfield, *Russian Fascism—Traditions, Tendencies, Movements,* (Armonk, New York and London, England: M. E. Sharpe, 2001) p. 191.

to Moscow where he became a prominent collaborator of Dugin's *Arktogeya* (Northern Land) association and "New University." He also became an adjunct professor at Moscow State University teaching Indian philosophy. Mamleev has been called "a representative of the aesthetics of evil," and describes in his cryptic novels scenes of human perversion and degradation. After Mamleev's emigration, the circle started, in the late 1970s, calling itself "Black Order of the SS," and its leader Evgenii Golovin (b. 1936) *Reichsführer SS*. Golovin, a poet, philosopher, translator, literary critic and mystic, had studied philology at Moscow State University, and gained, as a student, access to the closed section of the USSR's largest, Lenin Library.[50]

Umland's pithy summary of the character of the leadership of the "Yuzhinskii circle" already reveals a point which has been a source of grave concern for many who have studied and debated the doctrines of Aleksandr Dugin: a blending of mysticism and fascination with fascism or Nazism appear to have been significant characteristics of the circle. Still, according to published accounts, the circle was marked by debauchery; in Sedgwick's words: "The closest Golovin's circle came to action was that occasionally they would become very drunk. What Dugin later called 'excess in all forms' was seen as a form of revolt."[51]

However, the doctrines of the circle are of vastly greater significance than its debauched "excesses"; the "Yuzhinskii circle" is of enduring significance not because of its purported propensity to drunken debauchery mingled with

---

50   ibid., p. 146.

51   Mark Sedgwick, *Against the Modern World—Traditionalism and the Secret Intellectual History of the Twentieth Century*, (Oxford and New York: Oxford University Press, 2004) p. 223.

Nazi fetishism; instead, it is the doctrine which resided at the heart of the circle which should be searched for its enduring significance, for it was within the circle that Dugin acquired his enduring fixation with Traditionalism and the occult:

> In this circle, Golovin was progressively propagating occultism, esotericism, the 'integral Traditional' works of René Guénon and other authors and, later, Conservative Revolutionary and fascist classics. Golovin's 'faction' was characterised by 'a philosophy of denial of the surrounding reality as something evil, hostile, erroneous and artificial'. As soon as the modern world was diagnosed as chaotic and decadent, his followers started asking themselves 'when exactly the humanity had "strayed from God", and what needed to be done to return to "the Golden age"'.[52]

This brief synopsis of the teachings of the Golovin circle provides a fascinating summary of an entire system of thought, in that it explains the Traditionalist underpinning of Dugin's worldview, and it appears to establish the circle as one which was more Hermetic[53] than Gnostic, in the strict sense of the term. The Gnostic believes that the world itself is evil and "the material world was only devised to be the prison of the soul." However, for the Hermeticist, "The human body is not

52   Anton Shekhovtsov, "The Palingenetic Thrust of Russian Neo-Eurasianism: Ideas of Rebirth in Aleksandr Dugin's Worldview," *Totalitarian Movements and Political Religions,* December 2008 (9:4) p. 498.

53   Hermeticism (or Hermetism) is a body of doctrines derived, in whole or in part, from the purported writings of Hermes Trismegistus. (See, for example, the works included in Brian P. Copenhaver, *Hermetica* [Cambridge and New York: Cambridge University Press, 1992]. For an analysis of Hermetical doctrines during the 15th and 16th century Renaissance, see James D. Heiser, *Prisci Theologi and the Hermetic Reformation in the Fifteenth Century* [Malone, Texas: Repristination Press, 2011].)

40

the soul's prison devised by the bad demiurge and his evil powers but it is 'a beautiful and divine image' ... representing the utmost of God's creative power."[54] For the Gnostic, the world is simply a place from which one seeks to escape; for the Hermetic believer, the world is a place to be restored.[55] At the same time, the appeal to a return to a "Golden age" is a phantasm of Greek thought which extends at least as far back as Hesiod (ca. B.C. 750–650) and was caught up in the notion of recurring cycles of "ages"—a cycle which was fundamentally fatalistic in nature, since man could no more avoid the change of "ages" than he could change the seasons of the year. The search for a new "Golden Age" which could be initiated and sustained by human effort became a concern of the Renaissance, and in the Renaissance conception of the "Golden Age" one perceives the form of attainable age which the Golovin circle apparently sought.[56] Thus, with the circle's reliance on Western Traditionalists and its notion of the "Golden Age," the fundamentally Western origins of Dugin's thought begin to become apparent. And the ongoing ideological appeal of laboring toward a new "Golden Age" has led Dugin to laud individuals whose ideology he would otherwise reject, such as that of American Anarchist 'philosopher' John Zerzan.[57]

54   Roelof van den Broek, "Gnosticism and Hermetism in Antiquity—Two Roads to Salvation," in *Gnosis and Hermeticism from Antiquity to Modern Times,* ed. by Roelof van den Broek and Wouter J. Hanegraaff (Albany: State University of New York Press, 1998) p. 10.

55   The preponderance of 'Hermetical' writings being works concerned with alchemy confirms this point: alchemical Hermeticism seeks to convert the nature of the elements, while philosophical/religious Hermeticism seeks to convert the nature of man and society.

56   For an examination of the notion of the "Golden Age," see James Heiser, *A Time for Every Purpose Under Heaven* (Malone, Texas: Repristination Press, 2012), p. 53–70.

57   "His positive attitude toward 'neo-Luddites' also determines Dugin's respect toward John Zerzan, an American anarchist and primitivist

It is also apparent that Dugin's membership in the Golovin circle quickly provided an outlet and focus for his intellectual capabilities: Although he had only joined the circle in 1980, by the following year he had made a Russian translation of one of the seminal Traditionalist works—Julius Evola's *Pagan Imperialism (1928)*.[58] According to his online autobiographical notes,[59] Dugin also translated Guénon's *The Spiritist Fallacy (L'erreur spirite)*, and performed research in the area of "the Hermetic tradition and poetry" between 1982 and 1984. In 1991, Dugin also translated Guénon's *The Crisis of the Modern World*.[60] As will be discussed later, it is the contention of this author that Traditionalism is the most significant factor defining Dugin's ideology: Eurasianism is simply the political expression of his Traditionalist doctrine.

---

philosopher, who became known to a wider public after the trial of Theodore Kaczynski (also known as 'the Unibomber')... In spite of the obvious antagonism and innate conflict between radical left-wing anarchism and fascism, Dugin does not hesitate to refer to Zerzan because of the strong palingenetic sentiment expressed in the work of the latter. The idea behind Zerzan's anarcho-primitivism is that of the recovery of a 'Golden Age' of natural harmony and simple way of life by 'dismantling' the present technology-based modernity and 'unmaking of civilization' itself. ... Dugin disregards this anarcho-primitivist antithesis to his own doctrine just as he ignores the entire essence of anarcho-primitivism, implying that its only 'healthy element' is the idea of the abolition of the liminoid conditions of modernity, diagnosed as abnormal and malignant, to be followed by the immediate coming of a new 'Golden Age', regardless of the political or cultural content of this 'new world'." Anton Shekhovtsov, "The Palingenetic Thrust of Russian Neo-Eurasianism: Ideas of Rebirth in Aleksandr Dugin's Worldview," p. 497–498.

58   Mark Sedgwick, p. 222.

59   Available at http://dugin.ru/bio/ [Accessed May 8, 2014]

60   Andreas Umland, "Post-Soviet 'Uncivil Society' and the Rise of Aleksandr Dugin—A Case Study in Extraparliamentary Radical Right in Contemporary Russia (Ph.D. dissertation, Trinity College-Cambridge, 2007) p. 146–147.

Dugin and the KGB

It was during his association with the Golovin circle that Dugin purportedly had an encounter with the KGB which would change the course of his academic career. In his history of the Traditionalist movement, Sedgwick recounts the story of Dugin's expulsion from university:

> Golovin's circle seems to have attracted little official attention, although [Gaydar] Jamal reportedly was committed to a mental institution more than once (then a standard way of controlling dissidents). The KGB evidently came to tolerate such informal circles, within certain limits—limits which Dugin evidently exceeded. In 1983 the authorities learned of a party in a painter's studio where Dugin had played the guitar and sung what he called "mystical anti-Communist songs," and Dugin was briefly detained. The KGB found forbidden literature in his room, principally books by Alexander Solzhenitsyn and Mamleyev ... Dugin was expelled from the Institute of Aviation where he was then studying. He found employment as a street sweeper and continued reading in the Lenin Library with a forged reader's card.[61]

However, the biography of Aleksandr Dugin is often confusing when it comes to certain details; thus, for example, Umland cites "another biography of Dugin [which] says that, after his expulsion from the Aviation Institute, he started working in a KGB archive where he gained access to, and read large amounts of, forbidden literature on Masonry, fascism and paganism."[62] It would seem improbable that a man whose first attempt at an academic career was terminated by the

---

61   Mark Sedgwick, p. 223.
62   Andreas Umland, "Aleksandr Dugin's transformation ... ," p. 145–146.

KGB would then enter the employ of that same agency—but in the labyrinthine machinations of the *oprichniki* of the Soviet state, almost anything seems possible.

However, the story of Dugin's expulsion from the Moscow Institute of Aviation is even more complex. When Dugin sought to defend a doctoral dissertation in 2000, the reaction of certain Russian intellectuals was markedly hostile; in fact, when Dugin's dissertation was submitted, it was greeted by a member of the faculty, Boris Rezhabek, with the following assessment of Dugin's intellectual history in *The Bulletin of the Russian Philosophical Society*:

> Aleksandr Dugin is a domestic self-taught thinker, enjoying broad popularity in the narrow circles of National Bolsheviks and their sympathizers, as he is an extremely exuberant writer. Having flunked out of the Moscow Institute of Aviation (although he likes to say that he was expelled for anti-Soviet activities), Dugin embarked upon a quest into the occult and sexual experience. This was not so good for his future – after he had adopted the role of an Orthodox and became a member of the Central Council of the National Patriotic Front "*Pamiat'*," they found what he is and kicked him away...[63]

Rezhabek's scathing assessment of Dugin's philosophical peregrinations highlights the curious tension between the constancy of his ideology and the highly changeable character of his political affiliations. Efforts to characterize the Russian political landscape in the aftermath of the collapse of the Soviet Union is an endeavor fraught with difficul-

---

63   translation provided in Anastasia Mitrofanova, *The Politicization of Russian Orthodoxy—Actors and Ideas,* (Stuttgart: Ibidem-Verlag, 2005) p. 156–7. As of April 30, 2014, Rezhabek's entire article is available on line at http://lebed.com/2001/art2744.htm .

44

ties—especially when attempting to do so by means of comparison with Western categories of political thought. Still, in the assessment of this author, there is the appearance of a shift between organizations which would be considered either 'hard Right' and/or 'hard Left' to a self-conscious assertion of occupying the 'Center' in the progression of Dugin's political affiliations. Indeed, the shifts in Dugin's affiliations, and his eventual development of his notion of a "fourth political theory."[64]

Dugin and Pamyat' (1987–1989)

Dugin's first noteworthy affiliation was with the *Pamyat'* (*Pamiat'*) movement in the latter days of the Soviet Union. *Pamyat'* takes its name from the Russian word for "Memory" and, in that regard, it seems to be a memory of some of the worst tendencies in Russian culture before the revolutions of 1917, because *Pamyat'* has been seen as a "successor"[65] to the Black Hundred movement which spread throughout much of Russia in the last years of the tsars.

In the assessment of Walter Laqueur—whose history of the Black Hundred and its legacy remains vital reading for any student of their grim legacy—the Black Hundred "are a unique phenomenon in the history of twentieth-century politics"[66] and they were a phenomenon distinguished by criminality and anti-Semitism:

Count Witte, the former prime minister, wrote in his memoirs that "the Union was a body made up of plain thieves and hooligans": "The aims of the Black Hundred are usually selfish and of the lowest character. Their stomach and pockets dictate their aspirations.

---

64   Alexander Dugin, *The Fourth Political Theory* (2012).
65   Walter Laqueur, *Black Hundred—The Rise of the Extreme Right in Russia,* (New York: HarperCollins, 1993) p. 102.
66   ibid., p. 16.

They are typical murderers from the dark alleys." ...

The Black Hundred have entered history mainly as the perpetrators of the anti-Jewish pogroms of 1905–1906. ... There were three hundred victims of the pogrom in Odessa; a hundred and twenty were killed in Yetakerinoslav, forty-six in Kiev, eighty in Bialystok (in 1906), not counting the thousands injured. Altogether, there were some seven hundred such pogroms ...[67]

Although Laqueur observes that there is "no certainty with regard to Pamyat's origins" the name was adopted in 1983, having been "inspired by the novel *Pamyat* by Chivilikhin, which had been published one year earlier."[68] Like the "Yuzhinskii circle," *Pamyat'* appears to have arisen from various "patriotic groups" and "circles of book-lovers" which had existed since the 1970s; but *Pamyat'* found a common voice—at least for awhile—when Dmitri Vasiliev (Vasil'ev) joined it in 1984.

According to Laqueur, *Pamyat'* (like the Black Hundred before it) joined its 'patriotism' to large doses of anti-Semitism: "Its main propaganda theme ... was soon overtaken by an anti-Jewish campaign... The *Protocols of the Elders of Zion* became the most frequently quoted document in Pamyat propaganda."[69] Under the leadership of Vasiliev, the character of the organization was unmistakable; much of the organization's meetings were devoted to "short speeches on subjects such as the systematic destruction of national monuments, above all in Moscow; the responsibility was put on 'Zionist' architects acting in close association with foreign Masonic enemies of Mother Russia. The stage was set for the appearance of Vasiliev, who would talk for one to three hours

---

67   ibid., p. 20, 21.
68   ibid., p. 204–205.
69   ibid., p. 205.

46

and even longer."[70]

Given the implicit political propensities of *"Reichsführ-er SS.* Golovin," it is perhaps little surprise that Dugin was purportedly encouraged by Golovin to join *Pamyat'*.[71] Dugin joined *Pamyat'* in 1987, and soon assumed a key role within the organization, serving on the Central Council from late 1988 into 1989.[72] However, for as quickly as Dugin rose within the ranks of *Pamyat*, his departure was just as sudden, with Vasiliev referring to him as a "kike-mason"[73] after his departure in 1989.

According to Shekhovtsov, "Dugin joined 'Pamyat' and tried to change its course to that of 'Traditionalism' as he saw it."[74] If this assessment is correct, then it is hardly a surprise that the same organization ejected Dugin almost as quickly as it had elevated him to a position of prominence: the 'tradition' which was important to the leaders (and supporters) of *Pamyat'* was far removed from that of Traditionalism. *Pamyat'* was (in a fashion not atypical in Rightist organizations) quickly divided by petty squabbling and factionalism.[75] The fascinating thing about *Pamyat'* is that it existed in the latter days of the Soviet Union without being officially suppressed by the Communist regime; in fact, "Support for Pamyat came from

---

70   Laqueur, p. 207.

71   Andreas Umland, "Aleksandr Dugin's transformation ... ," p. 147.

72   John B. Dunlop, "Aleksandr Dugin's Foundations of Geopolitics," *Demokratizatsiya*, 12:1 (Winter 2004).

73   Andreas Umland, "Aleksandr Dugin's transformation ... ," p.147.

74   Anton Shekhovtsov, "The Palingenetic Thrust of Russian Neo-Eurasianism: Ideas of Rebirth in Aleksandr Dugin's Worldview," p. 498.

75   "To retrace all the splits and mergers that occurred on the extreme right would be nearly impossible; they were as frequent as those on the left. Splits occurred for a great variety of reasons, personal and ideological, and there was no Hitler or Mussolini on the political horizon in 1988–1989 capable of uniting the various sects." (Laqueur, p. 210.)

highly placed individuals in the Central Committee, the KGB, and the armed forces; there was more assistance on the regional level."[76]

Arctogaia[77] and Dugin's contacts with the Nouvelle Droite

Following his failure to evangelize *Pamyat'* to the cause of Traditionalism, Dugin began a period of outreach to the European 'New Right' (especially the French *Nouvelle Droite*). In connection with these efforts, his EON publishing house which he established in 1988 was transformed in 1991 into the "Historico-Religious Association *Arktogeia* (Northern land)" which became "a Russian 'node' of the broad ENR [European New Right] network."[78]

Dugin's outreach to the *Nouvelle Droite* was a natural choice: many of the French New Rightists had been influenced by Traditionalism (though perhaps not to the same degree as Dugin) and both Dugin and the New Right owed a particular debt to the anti-Modernist thought of the 1920s and '30s. In fact, the *Nouvelle Droite* seem to have developed an interest in Traditionalism around the same time that Dugin began his own study.[79]

---

76   Laqueur, p. 207.

77   Apart from quotations from sources which favor other spellings, we will use "Arctogaia" for Dugin's organization, since this is the English transliteration which he has adopted.

78   Anton Shekhovtsov, "Aleksandr Dugin's Neo-Eurasianism: The New Right *à la Russe*," in *Religion Compass* 3/4 (2009) p. 700.

79   "From the early 1980s, the ND devoted great intellectual energy to the Traditionalist school. ... In addition, a Traditionalist current emerged as a distinctive tendency within the ND. From the late 1970s onwards, this shift toward Traditionalism was discernible in a marked radical antimodernism within the words of Alain de Benoist, in particular his *L'Empire intérieur* (*The Inner Empire*). De Benoist was particularly influenced by Oswald Spengler (1880–1936) and Julius Evola, as well as his guiding star, Friedrich Nietzsche. Alain de Benoist elaborated 'new conservative' arguments, including the borrowing of

According to Dunlop, Dugin's first contacts with the *Nouvelle Droite* occurred in 1989 during a visit to the West and that he "became a fascist theorist" on account of these contacts:

> In 1989, taking advantage of increased opportunities to visit the West, Dugin spent most of the year traveling to Western European countries. While there, he strengthened ties with leading figures of the European New Right, such as Frenchman Alain de Benoist and Belgian Jean-Francois Thiriart. These contacts led to Dugin's "belated reconciliation" with the USSR, just as that state was approaching its final demise. It appears that, largely as a result of these contacts with the European Nouvelle Droite, Dugin became a fascist theorist. On the subject of Dugin's indubitable fascist orientation, Stephen Shenfield has written: "Crucial to Dugin's politics is the classical concept of the 'conservative revolution' that overturns the post-Enlightenment world and installs a new order in which the heroic values of the almost forgotten 'Tradition' are renewed. It is this concept that identifies Dugin unequivocally as a fascist."[80]

However, given the propensities of the Golovin circle, perhaps it might be best to say that Dugin's contacts with the New Right were more in the fashion of the discovery of 'kindred spirits'—at least in certain regards—who were able to help him expand on lines of thought which were already part of the Evolian Traditionalism which rests at the heart of his world view. Umland notes that Mamleyev may have facilitat-

---

a number of concepts derived from Evola." Stéphane François, "The *Nouvelle Droite* and 'Tradition'" in *Journal for the Study of Radicalism*, 8:1 (2014), p. 93.

80   John B. Dunlop, "Aleksandr Dugin's Foundations of Geopolitics," in *Demokratizatsiya* 12:1 (Winter 2004)

ed Dugin's contacts with the New Right, and emphasizes that these contacts developed into a reciprocal collaboration:

> ... Dugin met a number of ultra-nationalist European publicists including the Frenchman Alain de Benoist, the Belgian Jean-François Thiriart, and Italian Claudio Mutti. Possibly, Dugin was able to establish contacts with some of them thanks to the help of Mamleev who, at that time, must have lived in Paris. Later, these men, together with other, similarly oriented theorists, visited Dugin in Moscow, and participated to one degree or another in his various projects. In 1991, Dugin published a book called *Continente Russia* in Mutti's Italian publishing house. According to a further source, the Golovin circle had also contacts to the French publishing house called *Vivrism*, and to a Paris philosophical group around Tat'yana Goricheva.[81]

The influence of the Dugin's *Nouvelle Droite* contacts can be seen both in the name which he bestowed on his own organization—*Arctogaia*—and on his publication— *Elementy*—which took its name directly from the *Nouvelle Droite* publication, *Elements*. From its first issue in 1992, *Elementy* demonstrated Dugin's ability to draw influential Russians to his cause, with "texts by three generals who were then heads of department at the Academy of the General Staff."[82] *Elementy* also provided a forum within Russia in which New Rightists could address Russian Traditionalists and other extremists.[83]

81   Umland, "Aleksandr Dugin's transformation ... ," p. 147.

82   Laruelle, p. 3.

83   "As early as 1991 the journals *Den'* and *Elementy'* printed roundtable discussions in which leading West European New Rightists and national Bolsheviks, such as Alain de Benoist and Jean Thiriart, discussed the prospects of a Euro-Eurasian military partnership with representatives of the Russian military command and national-conservative politicians, such as Zyuganov, who later became chairman

However, de Benoist attempted to distance himself from Dugin in 1993 "after a virulent French and German press campaign against the 'red-and-brown threat in Russia.'"[84] Dugin's role leading up to helping found the National Bolshevik Party was probably the most problematic aspect of his endeavors, from de Benoist's perspective. However, as Laruelle notes, Dugin is also a more committed Traditionalist than de Benoist: "Indeed, de Benoist makes only partial use of Traditionalism, whereas Dugin draws on the whole body of that doctrine. Conversely, de Benoist is strongly attracted to Heidegger's philosophy, while Dugin does not find it congenial."[85] However, since the time of Laruelle's monograph, it is clear that there has been a rapprochement between Dugin and the *Nouvelle Droite*: Dugin's first major work addressed primarily to the Western world—*The Fourth Political Theory*—has been published by Arktos Media, Limited, a publishing house with caters to a Traditionalist/New Right audience, which describes itself, in part, as follows:

> Arktos has established itself as the principal publisher in English of the writings of the European "New Right" school of political thought (including original translations of works by its luminaries Alain de Benoist, Guillaume Faye and Pierre Krebs). We have also issued the first translations into English of the prominent Russian geopolitical thinker Alexander Dugin, who has served as an adviser to Vladimir Putin, as well as several works by the noted Italian traditionalist philosopher, Julius Evola.[86]

of the Communist Party (CPRF), and Yegor Ligachev, Gorbachev's main adversary." Markus Mathyl, "The National-Bolshevik Party and Arctogaia: two neo-fascist groupuscules in the post-Soviet political space," in *Patterns of Prejudice,* 36:3 (2002), p. 69.
84   Laruelle, p. 13.
85   ibid.
86   http://www.arktos.com/about/about-arktos.html   [Accessed

Arctogaia is Dugin's most enduring outlet for dissemi-
nating his views. Described as both a "think-tank"[87] and as
a "publishing house,"[88] The name of *Arctogaia* gives homage
to two men—Jörg Lanz von Liebenfels (1874–1954) and Guido
von List (1848–1919)—linked with the mystical racialist mad-
ness which spread in early twentieth century Germany. Lanz's
"theozoological" theory directly assaulted the humanity of
the non-Aryans and framed the struggle between Aryans and
non-Aryans in terms of a Gnostic dualism. In Gardell's words:
Merging Theosophy and Gnosticism with anthropolo-
gy and zoology, Lanz formulated the "theozoological"
theory as the "scientific" basis of a dualistic religion
in which Aryans and non-Aryans were identified as
carnal representations of the metaphysical principles
of good and evil locked in a battle for world dominion.
Lanz believed that the blond, blue-eyed Aryan was descended from an omniscient divine race that originally populated Arktogäa, a mythic Aryan motherland in
the North Pole region. When Aryan women engaged
in sexual relations with "daemon" races, the original
race lost its superhuman powers.[89]

In his *magnum opus*, *The Occult Roots of Nazism*, Nicholas Goodrick-Clarke directly connects "Lanz's neo-gnostic religion"
and his plans for the disposal of the 'inferior races' to plans
implemented within Nazi Germany: "The similarity between
Lanz's proposals and the later practices of Himmler's SS *Leb-*

May 8, 2014]
87   Mathyl, p. 64.
88   John B. Dunlop, "Aleksandr Dugin's Foundations of Geopolitics," in *Demokratizatsiya* 12:1 (Winter 2004)
89   Mattias Gardell, *Gods of the Blood—The Pagan Revival and
White Separatism,* (Durham, North Carolina: Duke University Press,
2003) p. 22.

ensborn maternity organization, and the Nazi plans for the disposal of the Jews and the treatment of the enslaved Slav populations in the East, indicate the survival of these mental reflexes over a generation."[90] As early as 1893, Guido van List began an effort to revive Odin (Wotan) worship on the basis of information gleaned from the Norse sagas and elsewhere, and he eagerly received numerous aspects of Lanz's "racist occultism," including "the manichaean struggle between the master-races (the Ario-Germans) and the slave races (non-Aryans) and a theory about the original homeland of the Aryans, a vanished polar continent called Arktogäa."[91]

It would appear that Dugin does not attempt to present the name of his Arctogaia organization as anything other than one which is in homage to von List and Lanz. In fact, the website associated with *The Fourth Political Theory* reprints an article which asserts:

> During the early 1990's, Dugin founded his own publishing house, named "Arktogeya." This name was borrowed from that of the publishing house of German racist writer Guido von List (1848-1918). It combines the ancient Greek words *arktos* (north) and *gea* or *gaia* (land), a reference to the vanished polar con-

90   Nicholas Goodrick-Clarke, *The Occult Roots of Nazism,* (New York: New York University Press, 1992) p. 97. Gardell shares this assessment: "To restore Aryan supremacy, Lanz developed a program with striking similarities to the national socialist policies that were to come: an Aryan revolution was necessary to clear society of degeneracy; inferior races were to be exterminated, deported, or enslaved; enforced eugenics would improve the race, castrating the inferior element and actively supporting the reproduction of the superior; Aryan females were to be assigned to breeding convents and matched to an elite of Aryan studs; racial rejuvenation would then empower the Aryan god-men to launch a world war to exterminate the racial enemy; securing the Aryan birthright to sufficient *lebensraum* would lay the foundation of a millenarian reich of Aryan supremacy." (Gardell, p. 22.)
91   Goodrick-Clarke, p. 55.

tinent that was supposedly the original home of the Aryans.[92]

And it is clear from Dugin's "Arctogaia Manifesto" that he subscribes to the notion of such a mythical polar continent and believes it to have relevance for an elite portion of mankind today:

> Literally "Arctogaia" means "The North Land". A mythical continent, that in former days was situated on the North Pole, but long ago disappeared from physical reality and so from short-lived human memory. Together with it disappeared, vanished a spiritual axis of Being, the World Tree that gave to all traditions and religions a light-bearing and operative-tranformative sense.[93] ...
>
> The men of Arctogaia are utmost not numerous and misunderstood, utterly misplaced in modern world, detached and differential.They totally disclaim all the apocaliptic [sic] realm of modernity and in the same way totally affirm the alternative world, world of Tradition, world of Pole, world of Being, WORLD OF ARCTOGAIA.
>
> Anticrist [sic] besides theological also has geopolitical, immanently social meaning. It is evident today that the most "perfect" and "complete" form of the historical realisation of this sinister personage is the liberal West, that ideology and that system which has won in the cold war, the war against USSR and settled everywhere the foundations of the planet domi-

---

92   John B. Dunlop, "Aleksandr Dugin's Foundations of Geopolitics," republished at: www.4pt.su/content/aleksandr-dugin's-foundations-geopolitics [accessed April 25, 2014]

93   Note: Dugin thus links the Norse pagan notion of *Yggdrassil* (the World Tree) with the "Primordial Tradition" of the Traditionalist movement.

nation in the form of the "new world order".

The resistance to the power of the atlantic "evil empire", USA and the liberal capitalistic model sould [sic] be greeted in all forms and at all combinations. Everyone who bids the defiance to anticrist [sic] (even if he doesn't suspect of the real quality of the entity he deals with), is anyway worth of respect and earns our sympathy and solidarity. ...

Arctogaia, the elite of the absent continent, the princes of the non-existent country, spreads in all directions. This is a circular aggression of the potential which will soon be the actual. ...

For the people of Arctogaia every man is a potential Angel and his consciousness is a flower.

They are fighting with us (succesfully [sic]). We rise against them (but almost always lose).

This is a logic of history. Until we exist it is not finished (whatever Fucuyama would say).

But a moment will come, and we'll overpower them . But this victory will be the last and the final.

Endkampf und Endsieg.

There won't be any time.

Join us, because tomorrow it will be late [sic].[94]

Dugin's "Manifesto" offers a delightful example of the flavor of his rants against the West, in general, and against the United States, in particular. The elite of Arctogaia are cast in a "circular aggression" against Antichrist, that is, the United States; the invocations of the "apocalyptic" character of this "Endkampf/Final Struggle" highlights the occult character of his thought, with a radical dualism between the "sinister per-

---

94   http://arctogaia.com/public/eng2.htm [Accessed May 8, 2014. According to the webpage, the text was last updated on September 20, 1998]

sonage" of the West and the "angels" of Arctogaia. No compromise between powers is possible: once one has labeled one's enemy as the "Antichrist," all negotiations have presumably long since drawn to a close. It is worth observing that the last editing of this "Manifesto" was in September 1998; that is, a year after publication of Dugin's influential geopolitical work, *The Foundations of Geopolitics*. Even momentary reflection on the ranting apocalyptic language of the "Manifesto" is worthy of comparison with the political processes of Western civilization: How long could any significant Western 'expert' on geopolitics or international relations survive publishing something as fevered as the "Arctogaia Manifesto"? And yet, far from being damaged by such fanaticism, in that same year, *Arctogaia* launched its "New University" to spread occultism and Traditionalism; in the words of Mitrofanova:

> The function of the university is to teach such disciplines as traditionalism, theology, history of religions, metaphysics, hermetism, geopolitics, sociology, philology, history, ethnology, psychology, political science and conspirology. The New University does not aim at educating the public; it is rather a facility attracting people interested in mysticism and occultism.[95]

Dugin and the National Bolshevik Party (1993–1998)

Following his involvement with the *Pamyat'* movement, Dugin continued his efforts to influence the Russian "patriotic" movement by means of dissemination of Traditionalist doctrine, and the expression of that doctrine in Eurasianist practice. This meant not only working on building his own organization, *Arctogaia*, and strengthening his ties with ideological fellow travelers in the European New Right; it also involved advancing to the next level of his involvement with

95   Mitrofanova, p. 162.

the Russian far-right by means of the *Den'/Zavtra* newspaper and the formation of the National Bolshevik Party. Laqueur took note of *Den'* when he wrote his book on Russian extremism in the immediate aftermath of the fall of the Soviet Union. *Den'*, he observed, marked a change from the status quo when it came to extremist publications:

> Whereas the sectarian literature of 1989–1991 was written for a barely literate public, the weekly *Den*, which came into being in 1991 as the flagship of the 'spiritual opposition,' clearly had middlebrow (if not highbrow) political and literary ambitions from the beginning. But not many months passed before it began to lower its sights, what with the publication of excerpts from Adolf Hitler, the *Protocols* [*of the Elders of Zion*], and 'conspiratology' of the most ludicrous kind. The articles were written in better Russian than that of the sectarian sheets, but there was no less abstruseness or madness.[96]

Of course, Dugin literally wrote the book on "conspirology" (his book with that title—*Conspirologiya*[97]—was published in 1992 and reprinted in 2005), and he quickly became a prolific writer for *Den'*—and then for its successor publication, *Zavtra*, after *Den'* was banned in 1993. It was Dugin's involvement with *Den'* which helped gain him an 'audience' for his occult worldview:

> *Zavtra* serves as a nursery for the emerging leaders of political Orthodoxy, giving them an opportunity to reach nation-wide audience. This was the case of Aleksandr Dugin. He was known to a tiny circle of Moscow counter-culture intellectuals and acquired

96   Laqueur, p. 265.
97   Available online at http://my.arcto.ru/public/consp/consp1. htm [Accessed May 9, 2014]

nation-wide popularity thanks to his publications in *Zavtra* where he edited an inset "Invasion: The National Bolshevik Territory" and then "Eurasian Invasion."[98]

Den/Zavtra thus helped provide an audience for Dugin, and helped to pave the way for the creation of the National Bolshevik Party, as Dugin became an increasingly-prominent intellectual on the right and as he began to shape the terms of political discourse within the ranks of the Russian Right:

> Dugin has influenced the post-Soviet "patriotic" movement ideologically to a greater degree than any other nationalist publicist, especially through his association with Alexander Prokhanov, the editor and publisher of *Zavtra* (previously *Den'*). Dugin's Eurasianist writings in *Den'/Zavtra* gave the "patriotic" opposition the outline of an ideology that became the basis for Prokhanov's efforts to unite the "Reds" (mainly grouped in the Russian Communist Party) and "Whites" (the nationalists) around Russia's historical Eurasianist mission. Dugin's vocabulary ("Atlanticism," "Eurasianism," "mondialism") permeated the discourse of the "patriotic" movement: Prokhanov, for instance, once summed up the editorial line of his newspaper as the promotion of Eurasianism, which he defined as the union of Slavs and Turks, Muslims and Orthodox.[99]

It was during this same time period that Dugin worked with Eduard Limonov to found the National Bolshevik Party

---

98   Anastasia V. Mitrofanova, *The Politicization of Russian Orthodoxy—Actors and Ideas,* (Stuttgart: Ibidem-Verlag, 2005) p. 109.
99   Wayne Allensworth, "Dugin and the Eurasian controversy" in *Russian Nationalism and the National Reassertion of Russia,* ed. by Marlène Laruelle (London and New York: Routledge, 2009) p. 105.

(NBP); the 1993–4 time period marked a shift in Dugin's efforts away from seeking to influence Gennady Zyuganov's Communist Party of the Russian Federation (CPRF).[100] Dugin apparently found himself 'reconciled with Soviet reality' right at the moment when the Soviet Union vanished forever; he thus began to associate with "statist patriots" for a while during period between his association with *Pamyat'* and his efforts to start the NBP.[101]

The NBP emerging through the efforts of Limonov and Dugin in the immediate aftermath of the establishment of *Arctogaia*, and the two organizations overlapped in their efforts (at least for a time), with Dugin and his organization provided the ideological substance at the heart of the NBP.[102] Thus, in the words of Eduard Limonov, who was appointed the leader of the National Bolshevik Party, Dugin was "the 'Cyril and Methodius' of fascism, since he brought Faith and knowledge about it to our country from the West."[103] Mathyl agrees with this assessment: "The entire ideology of the NBP can be

---

100   "From 1993–4, Dugin moved away from the Communist spectrum and became the ideologist for the new National Bolshevik Party" (Laruelle, *Aleksandr Dugin: A Russian Version of the European Radical Right?*, p. 2). It is worth noting that Laruelle also considers Dugin to have had a significant impact on Zyuganov's geostrategic thinking: "[Zyuganov's] book *Russia after the year 2000: A Geopolitical Vision for a New State* was directly inspired by Dugin's ideas on the distinctiveness of Russian geopolitical 'science' and his idea that Russia's renewal provides the only guarantee of world stability." (ibid.)

101   Stephen D. Shenfield, *Russian Fascism—Traditions, Tendencies, Movements,* (Armonk, New York and London, England: M.E. Sharpe, 2001) p. 192.

102   "The intellectual father of the NBP is considered to be Aleksandr Dugin…" Mathyl, p. 65.

103   Laruelle, *Aleksandr Dugin: A Russian Version of the European Radical Right?*, p. 2. SS. Cyril and Methodius are remembered as the "Apostles to the Slavs" for their ministry among the Slavs in the ninth century.

traced to the activities of Dugin and the Arctogaia group."[104]

Given the importance of Dugin's ideology for the NBP, his essay entitled, "The metaphysics of national-bolshevism,"[105] is extremely helpful for discerning his understanding of the relationship between the NBP and Traditionalism. Dugin observes that "the term 'national-bolshevism' can mean several quite different things." What he wants his readers to understand is that what he means by "National Bolshevism" can best be understood in the context of Karl Popper's *Open Society and its Enemies*, which Dugin describes as Popper's "inestimable contribution" in which "Popper proposes a rather convincing model, according to which all the types of society are roughly divided into two main kinds".[106] Dugin places the tenets of "national-bolshevism" as being of that type which are "defined by Popper as a 'hostile to open society'":

> The most felicitous and full definition of national-bolshevism will be as follows: "National-bolshevism

104   Mathyl, p. 67.

105   http://arctogaia.com/public/eng-teor.htm [Accessed May 9, 2014] Please note that the English text is that which is available from the *Arctogaia* website. Dugin's spelling and grammar have been retained throughout, contrary to all aesthetic sensibilities, to retain the precise expression of his thought.

106   The present author believes that Eric Voegelin offers a more accurate assessment of Popper's work: "Popper is philosophically so uncultured, so fully a primitive ideological brawler, that he is not able even approximately to reproduce correctly the contents of one page of Plato. Reading is of no use to him; he is too lacking in knowledge to understand what the author says. ... Briefly and in sum: Popper's book is a scandal without extenuating circumstances; in its intellectual attitude it is the typical product of a failed intellectual; spiritually one would have to use expressions like rascally, impertinent, loutish; in terms of technical competence, as a piece in the history of thought, it is dilettantish, and as a result is worthless." (http://thephilosophyofscience.wordpress.com/2011/07/15/strauss-and-voegelin-on-popper/)

is a superideology [sic], common for all open society enemies." Not just one of the hostile to such society ideologies, but it is exactly its full conscious, total and natural antithesis. The national-bolshevism is a kind of an ideology, which is built on the full and radical denial of the individual and his central role; also, the Absolute, in which name the individual is denied, has the most extended and common sense.

Dugin thus apparently believes that National Bolshevism simply subsumes into itself *all* ideologies which oppose individualism, regardless of any hostilities which exist between such "close society" ideologies: "The national-bolsheviks were exactly the first to try grouping the different ideologies, hostile to 'open society', they revealed, as well as their ideological opponents, some common axis, uniting round itself all possible alternatives to individualism and to the individualism based society."

In this article, Dugin provides his "metaphysics" for both Bolshevism and nationalism. Dugin's interest in Karl Marx as the source for the metaphysics of Bolshevism appears to center in his "eschatological messianist scenario" and he likens Marx's intended transformation of society ("his aspiration to the magical transformation of the reality") to the labors of "the medieval alchemists"—a claim which probably speaks more clearly concerning Dugin's occultism than it does regarding the ideological content of Marxism.[107] Dugin declares:

> It is this Gnostic tendency of Marx and his predecessors was applied by the Russian bolsheviks, who were raised up in an environment, where the enigmatic

---

107   The reader is encouraged to remember Dugin's interest in Hermeticism and the focus of much of the extant Hermetical literature on alchemy.

forces of Russian sects, mysticism, national messiaism [sic], secret societies and passionate romantic characters of Russian rebels were being summoned against the alienated, temporal, degraded monarchic regime. "Moscow - Third Rome, Russian people is the God carrier, the nation of the All-man. Russia is destined to rescue the world. All those ideas impregnated Russian life, which had it in common with the esoterical [sic] plots incorporated in the Marxism. ...

The national-bolshevism takes turn of just such bolshevik tradition, the policy of the "right communism", which was originated by the ancient initiatic societies and spiritual doctrines in remote ages. Thus the economic aspect of communism is not diminished, is not denied, but is considered as a gear of the teurgic [sic, theurgic], magic practice, as a particular tool of a reality transformation.

In short, then, what Dugin proposes is that National Bolshevism takes from the "metaphysics" of Marxism a secret, initiatory Gnosticism and mysticism which seeks to accomplish a spiritual alchemy to transform society—National Bolshevism thus becomes a secret society bent on a theurgic, magic transformation of reality.

As if Dugin's metaphysics of Marxism were insufficiently mystical, his metaphysics of nationalism are possibly even more so, for here he introduces his belief in 'national angels' which determine the character and course of nations:

According to Tradition doctrine, the certain angel, the celestial being is appointed to look after each nation of the Earth. This angel is the given nation's history sense, being out of the time and the space, but being constantly present in all nation's historical peripetias. The mysticism of a nation is based

62

on this. Nation's angel isn't anything vague or senti-
mental, indistinctly dim. This is an intellectual, lighting [sic] being, "God's thought", as Gerder said. Its
structure one can see in nation's historical achieve-
ments, in social and religious institutes, which characterize the nation, in the national culture.

Dugin thus presents his geopolitical posture as one dictated
by the mystical sense of a 'war in heaven,' and there is no
doubt in his mind as to which nations are governed by the
'better angels,' and which most decidedly are not: "The angel
of Russia is discovered as the integration angel, as some special lighting being, seeking to teleologically unite other angelic beings inside itself, not obliterating their individuality,
but elevating it to the universal imperial scales." Speaking
teleologically—in other words, to the purpose for which the
other angels must ultimately serve—is for them to be united
into the angel of Russia. The "universal imperial" end of the
angel of Russia is to incorporate into itself all the 'good angels.' As for the West, a different angelic order is at work:

So, it is being gradually explained, the dualism between the East and the West, dubbed by the ethnic dualism: the land, "ideocratic" Russia (the Slavic world
plus other Eurasian nations) against the island "plu-
tocratic" Anglo-Saxon West. The angelic horde of Eurasia against the Atlantic capitalism armies. About the
true nature of Capital's "angel" (in Tradition its name
is "Mammon") one could easily guess...[108]

Again, as was seen in the "Arctogaia Manifesto," an irrecon-
cilable dualism directs Dugin's system, so that he literally de-
monizes his enemies. And Dugin credits Traditionalism for
this dualistic hermeutic:

108   The ellipsis is in the original.

... the main incentive of the 'open society enemies' and its most raging and consistent enemies, national-bolsheviks, is never based on the rationalist grounds. The works of traditionalists help in that most of all, first of all it is those of Rene Guenon and Julius Evola. Both Guenon and Evola expounded the mechanics of the cyclic process, in which the degradation of the earth element (and corresponding human consciousness), the civilization desacralization, and the modern "rationalism" with all its logical consequences is regarded as one of the last stages of degradation.

For Dugin, this reference to the "last stages" is important, given his propensity to repeatedly return to an eschatological significance to our times, and the conflict which he presents between the world powers in this age. The conclusion of his essay sets forth the notion that the world has precisely come to the final 'angelic' struggle, following in the aftermath of the defeat of fascism and the USSR: "The fascism fell first, then there was the last anti-liberal citadel turn, that of the USSR. At first sight, in 1991 the last page of the book of the geo-political confrontation with Mammon, the Atlantic West demon, the perverted 'cosmopolitical Capital's angel', is closed." But all is not lost: "The national-bolshevism is the 'open society enemies' last asylum, unless they want to persist in their outdated, not historically adequate and absolutely not effective doctrines." (This is Dugin's way of telling modern fascists and communists that they are wasting their time unless they enlist in the ranks of the 'national-bolsheviks': their time has come and gone.) For Dugin, the call of national-bolsheviks supplants all loyalties to fascist or communist ideologies:

> Beyond "rights" and "lefts", there's one and indivisible Revolution, in the dialectical triad "third

Rome - Third Reich - third International."

The realm of national-bolshevism, Regnum, their Empire of the End, this is the perfect accomplishment of the greatest Revolution of the history, both continental and universal one. It is the angels' return, heroes' resurrection, the heart's uprising against the reason's dictatorship. This last revolution is a concern of the acephal, the headless bearer of the cross, sickle and hammer, crowned by eternal sun fylfot.

Since Dugin's choice of terms is obscure, it is worth noting that the "eternal sun fylfot" is the swastika. The "Empire of the End" is acephal—headless—bearing the cross (Third Rome), hammer and sickle (Third International) and swastika (Third Reich)—defeating the demonic forces of the West by means of the Eurasian angels. In his assessment of this gnostic twaddle, the present author finds himself in agreement with the evaluation of National Bolshevism offered by Laruelle in her book, *Russian Eurasianism:*

Dugin's view of National Bolshevism rests largely on mystical foundations, which, once more reminds one of the original Fascists. He stresses the parallels between esotericism and political commitment, be it Fascist, Nazi, or Bolshevik; National Bolshevism is thus to him merely a politicized version of Traditionalism, the modernized expression of the messianic hopes that have existed in Russia since the fall of Constantinople in 1453. According to Dugin, it heralds "the Last Revolution—the work of an acephalous, headless bearer of cross, hammer, and sickle, crowned by the eternal swastika of the sun." Thus, for him, the most complete incarnation of the third way was German National Socialism, much more so than Mussolini's Italy or the interwar Russian exiles. He then points out parallels between "Third Rome, the Third Reich, the Third International," and he attempts to prove their common eschatological basis. For Dugin, the original triad of Father, Son, and Holy Spirit reveal to the initiated that the Third Reich, just like Third Rome, will be the kingdom of the Holy Spirit.[109]

As we will see later, Dugin's "kingdom of the Holy Spirit" marks his movement as one which should be called (using the term coined by Eric Voegelin) a "gnostic mass movement." Given the obvious importance which Dugin perceived to reside in his National Bolshevist doctrine, we understand the significance of his disagreements with Limonov which led to Dugin's decision to leave the NBP, just as his earlier falling out with Vasiliev led to his expulsion from *Pamyat'*. But, once again, Dugin displayed a certain feline propensity for 'landing on his feet.' Dugin left the NBP not because he abandoned the National Bolshevist ideology, but to preserve that ideology in a more advanced form.

The Foundations of Geopolitics and Dugin's Entrance into the 'Russian Mainstream'

In 1997, Dugin wrote *The Foundations of Geopolitics: Russia's Geopolitical Future*, a work which made it possible for him to increase his access to the mainstream of Russia's parliamentary structures.[110] According to Laruelle, *Foundations* "seems to have been written with the support of General Igor' Rodionov, who was minister of defense in 1996–97."[111] Between 1997 and 2000, the book had already been reissued four times. During this window of time, Dugin launched his

109   Marlène Laruelle, *Russian Eurasianism—An Ideology of Empire*, trans. by Mischa Gabowitsch (Baltimore: The John Hopkins University Press, 2008) p. 133-134.
110   ibid., p. 109.
111   ibid., p. 110.

66

"Center for Geopolitical Expertise" which (in Mitrofanova's words) had the "purpose of indoctrinating officials (and bringing monetary benefits)"[112] and which, in Dugin's words, "works simultaneously with the Presidential Administration, the Government of the Russian Federation, the Council of the Federation and the State Duma, [and] could become the Eurasian platform's analytical tool."[113]

In Umland's assessment[114] the writing of *Foundations* and the creation of the Center for Geopolitical Expertise provided Dugin with opportunity to resolve the "contradiction in Dugin's simultaneously groupuscular and Gramscian strategy"—which is to say, it provided an opportunity to ascend from the sectarian fringes of Russian society and to begin bringing his ideology into the corridors of power. Like *Pamyat'* before it, the National Bolshevik Party was of limited future utility, but it had opened up further opportunities. If this was indeed Dugin's strategy, it was highly successful:

Thus, the years 1998 to 2000 saw the transformation of Dugin's political leanings into a specific current that employs multiple strategies of entryism, targeting both youth counterculture and parliamentary structures. He succeeded in establishing himself as an adviser to the Duma's spokesman, the Communist Gennady Seleznev, and, in 1999, he became the chairman of the geopolitical section of the Duma's Advisory Council on National Security, dominated by Zhirinovsky's Liberal-Democratic Party (LDPR). ... Dugin also regularly publishes in *Krasnaya Zvezda*, the

---

112   Mitrofanova, p. 162.
113   quoted in Laruelle, *Russian Eurasianism*, p. 110.
114   Andreas Umland, "Toward an Uncivil Society? Contextualizing the Recent Decline of Extremely Right-Wing Parties in Russia," (Cambridge, MA: Weatherhead Center for International Affairs, Harvard University, 2002) p. 36.

army newspaper, and on Russian official Web sites.[115]

With the publication of *Foundations*, Dugin had found his entrance to the corridors of power. No longer limited to the fringes of Rightist thought and extremist parties, the stage was set for the next step in the development of an ideology which had been painted in broad strokes for the NBP: the ideology of Eurasianism.

---

115   Laruelle, *Russian Eurasianism,* p. 110.

Eurasianism—The "Armed Doctrine" of Traditionalism

Civilizations are cultural and religious communities—not ethnic-national ones.[116]

When one considers the arc of Dugin's intellectual and political career, one can be impressed by his shrewdness and sense of timing. At each step, Dugin's departure from an organization has signaled not a loss or a setback for his agenda, but has amounted to the steady advance of his influence. Prior to his separation from the National Bolshevik Party (NBP) and over the course of the next several years, Dugin's promotion of his *Foundations of Geopolitics* was a key element of preparing for the next step in his development. In 1999, Dugin launched a new monthly publication from his *Arctogaia* publishing house: *Evraziiskoe vtorzhenie* [*Eurasian Invasion*].[117] As noted previously, Dugin gained significant influence in 1999 when he became an advisor to Seleznev, the chairman of the Russian Duma, and when Vladimir Zhirinovsky made him chairman of the Duma's Advisory Council on National Security. Dugin thus had already made a significant advance in his political standing prior to Putin's election in March 2000.[118]

116   Dugin, *The Fourth Political Theory*, p. 165.
117   Stephen Shenfield, *Russian Fascism—Traditions, Tendencies, Movements*, p. 193.
118   As Mathyl observes: "Having risen to the position of official adviser to the president of the Russian parliament in 1998, Dugin then succeeded in establishing a relationship with the administration of the new president Putin by founding the broad, inclusive Eurasia movement in April 2001. Remarkably, he succeeded in doing so without breaking his close ties to western New Right and radical-right groups or removing his neo-fascist writings from the Internet." (p. 74) These facts remain unchanged in the 12 years since Mathyl wrote his article.

In 2000, Dugin submitted his Ph.D. dissertation to North-Caucasian Higher School Scientific Center—followed by his Dr. habilitat dissertation in Political Science in 2004 at the Rostov Juridical Institute of the Ministry of the Interior of the Russian Federation[119]—which helped solidify his academic credibility.[120] Dugin was thus ready for the election of a leader whom he could hope to influence—a leader who would steadily become less interested in peace (or even reasonable accommodation) with the West:

> Putin's election as president in March 2000 caused an even stronger shift in Dugin's political attitudes, as he began to move closer to country's [sic] new strong man.

> On 21 April 2001 he resolved to put his cards on the table and created a movement named *Evraziia,* of which he was elected president. During its founding convention, *Evraziia*—often described as a brainchild of presidential counsel Gleb Pavlovsky, who is close to Dugin—officially rallied to Putin and proposed to participate in the next elections as part of a government coalition.[121]

119   Andreas Umland, "Post-Soviet 'Uncivil Society' and the Rise of Aleksandr Dugin—A Case Study in Extraparliamentary Radical Right in Contemporary Russia (Ph.D. dissertation, Trinity College-Cambridge, 2007) p. 138, 139.

120   The need to acquire proof of academic qualifications was obviously a sensitive point for Dugin, who appears to have not possessed any advanced degree prior to this point. Mitrofanova relates: "On 5 November 1997, during Dugin's meeting with the students of the Moscow State University … he simply refused to answer a question about his educational background; at that moment he had no higher education at all." (p. 156) The only record this writer has found concerning Dugin's higher education between his removal from the Moscow Aviation Institute and his submission of his Ph.D. dissertation was Mitrofanova's reference to "a diploma from extra-mural department of the Novocherkassk Institute of Melioration Engineering". (p. 157)

121   Laruelle, *Aleksandr Dugin: A Russian Version of the European*

The timing of the founding of *Evraziia*—the Eurasia Movement—was launched as a platform for Dugin's ideology at a time which presumably served the interests of the new Russian president. Aside from Pavlovsky's purported involvement in its founding, the transformation of *Evraziia* into a political party in May 2002 was "publicly welcomed by Aleksandr Voloshin, then the head of the presidential administration, and Aleksandr Kosopkin, chief of the administration's Internal Affairs Department."[122] For his part, Dugin declared his support for Putin: "Speaking to the Political Council of *Evraziia* in 2001 Dugin insisted that 'true Eurasianism can only be achieved via Putin. What stands against Putin is pseudo-Eurasianism.'"[123] Looking back over the course of the intervening years, it is striking to see how Dugin's comments regarding Putin have been fulfilled. As Barbashin and Thoburn recently noted for *Foreign Affairs*:

> Since the early 2000s, Dugin's ideas have only gained in popularity. Their rise mirrors Putin's own transition from apparent democrat to authoritarian.

Radical Right?, p. 3.
122   Laruelle, *Russian Eurasianism*, p. 111.
123   Mitrofanova, p. 192. In a January 1, 2001 statement which called for the establishment of *Evraziia,* Dugin announced his loyalty to Putin, and his support for whatever "unpopular actions" Putin might be led to take: "We realise that today's authority in Russia, the President of Russia Vladimir Vladimirovic Putin requires help, support, solidarity, cohesion. … Here again we will be for the President fervently, radically, up to the end, not paying attention to small inaccuracies, accepting all hardships and difficulties, which will arise since Russia will seriously be set by the purpose of rescuing itself and all the rest of the world from the terrible threat creeping from the West. Anything more centrist than our unconditional and total support to the patriotic power-building of the authority (even in its most unpopular actions) simply could not be." Aleksandr Dugin, "Eurasia above all" rossia3.eu/eng/Eurasiaabove [Accessed May 4, 2014]

In fact, Putin's conservative turn has given Dugin a perfect chance to "help out" the Russian leader with proper historical, geopolitical, and cultural explanations for his policies. Recognizing how attractive Dugin's ideas are to some Russians, Putin has seized on some of them to further his own goals.[124]

However, given the circumstances of the founding of *Evraziia*, it seems far to say that Putin has been far from a passive recipient of Dugin's ideas; it would seem that he has been willing to extend his political credibility to them to provide a context in which they could grow in the Russian public square. Shenfield noted in 2001: "About fifty students in Moscow currently consider themselves his [Dugin's] followers."[125] While this figure clearly did not include his support in other cities and regions of Russia, it does raise the question of the means by which so many supporters were drawn so quickly to his movement in conjunction with the establishment of *Evraziia*.[126]

Coincidentally, the timing of *Evraziia*'s beginning also coincided with the 'beginning of the end' of the previous phase of Dugin's intellectual career, with the arrest of Eduard Limonov in April 2001 on "charges of illegal arms trading

124   Anton Barbashin and Hannah Thoburn, "Putin's Brain—Alexander Dugin and the Philosophy Behind Putin's Invasion of Crimea." www.foreignaffairs/com/articles/141080/anton-barbashin-and-hannah-thoburn/putins-brain [Accessed April 15, 2014]
125   Shenfield, p. 199.
126   "Dugin had quickly transformed his Eurasian movement into a party. This could not be done without at least indirect encouragement from above. The Congress and party organization required considerable funds and presumably the blessing of a friend in the Kremlin; most likely, direct financial support made it possible to engage in the venture." Dmitry Shlapentokh, Russian Elite Image of Iran: From the Late Soviet Era to the Present, (Carlisle, PA: Strategic Studies Institute, U.S. Army War College, 2009) p. 36.

and preparing for armed revolt in northern Kazakhstan".[127]
As Mathyl wrote in 2002:

> Limonov is charged with the preparation of an armed insurrection in North Kazakhstan where displeasure among the Russian minority regarding the sometimes discriminatory Kazakhstani government policy is particularly prevalent. Although Limonov earlier openly admitted such plans, many details remain unclear. One thing can be said with certainty: since 2001 a new form of pressure has been exerted on the NBP by judicial institutions, including attempts to implement an outright ban of the party.[128]

Limonov was released from Lefortovo Prison in 2003. Beginning in 2005, the NBP did go through a tumultuous period in the courts regarding its legal status; in November 2005 the Supreme Court of Russia upheld the ban on the NBP, which had been banned "on the grounds that it had violated the law on political parties by calling itself a 'party' without having official registration" (Limonov protested that the NBP had applied multiple times for standing as a political party, only to be declined for "trivial" reasons).[129] In July 2010, many members of the NBP launched a new political party, "The Other Russia."

The orderly formation of *Evraziia* was a marked contrast to the chaos which overtook the NBP. On May 30, 2002, *Evraziia* became a political party which Dugin defined as "radically centrist"—a nomenclature which Laruelle deems "springs from his Traditionalist attitude."[130] At the time of its

---

127   Mathyl, p. 74.
128   ibid.
129   "UPDATE: Russian Supreme Court upholds ban on National Bolshevik Party" (RIA Novosti) http://en.ria.ru/russia/20051115/42096057.html [Accessed May 12, 2014]
130   Laruelle, *Russian Eurasianism,* p. 111.

founding, Dugin's Eurasian Party boasted fifty-nine branches and a membership of more than 10,000 people. The founding of the Eurasian Party was hardly a challenge to Putin's authority: "The Kremlin has long tolerated, and even encouraged, the creation of such smaller allied political parties, which given Russian voters the sense that they actually do live in a democracy."[131]

Dugin's Eurasian ideology provided something which had been missing in Russian foreign policy since the collapse of the Soviet Union. The utter collapse of Marxism-Leninism as a coherent body of doctrine was hardly a recent development when Mikhail Gorbachev came to power; but the sudden implosion of Soviet power brought a speedy end to a totalitarian regime which many analysts had imagined only a few years earlier would be likely to endure for generations. The seeming-aimlessness of Russian foreign policy reflected the drift within Russian society as a whole. A Communist regime which had endeavored to present itself as omnipotent found itself impotent to maintain its power: when hardliners arranged a coup to retain power, the threat of excommunication by the Russian Orthodox patriarch—himself a man who had served the KGB for 33 years—was enough to bring about the final collapse of Soviet power in the early morning hours of August 21, 1991.[132]

In an article entitled "Main Principles of Eurasist Policy,"[133] Dugin describes three "reciprocally conflicting patterns of state strategy" which have contended for priority in the post-Soviet period. The first pattern "represents the

131   Barbashin and Thoburn.

132   John Garrard and Carol Garrard, *Russian Orthodoxy Resurgent—Faith and Power in the New Russia,* (Princeton and Oxford: Princeton University Press, 2008) p. 14–35.

133   "Main Principles of Eurasist Policy," www.4pt.su.k0.gfns.net/tr/node/30 [Accessed April 18, 2014]

inertial cliché of the Soviet (mainly later Soviet) period. ... This pattern is supported with the 'relevant' argument: «It worked earlier, it will work also now.»" The second pattern "is the liberal-democrat, pro-American one. It started taking shape with the beginning of 'perestroika' and became some kind of dominant ideology in the first half of the 1990s. ... The argument here too is rather simple: «It works for them, it will work for us too.»" However, in Dugin's assessment, neither of these ideologies could serve the interests of post-Soviet Russia. What was needed was the Eurasian ideology:

> As the two former orthodox patterns show their unfitness, eurasism becomes more and more popular. The Soviet pattern operates with obsolete political, economic and social realities, it exploits nostalgia and inertness, it lacks a sober analysis of the new international situation and the real development of world economic trends. The pro-American liberal pattern, in turn, can not be realised in Russia by definition, being an organic part of another civilisation, alien to Russia. This is well understood in the West too, where nobody disguises their preference to see not a prospering and safe Russia, but, on the contrary, a weakened Russia, submerged in the abyss of chaos and corruption.

As depressing as Dugin's reflexive paranoia regarding Western motivations and intentions regarding Russia may be, it is a paranoia which is inextricable from the Traditionalist anti-modernism at the heart of Eurasianism. Eurasianism is a doctrine which is built on perpetuating hostility toward many of the same nations which seven decades of Marxist-Leninist propaganda had taught the people to hate, but it changed the *motivation* for that hatred, abandoning the Bolshevik boilerplate about the 'class struggle' for a global struggle which rests at the very heart of the geography of Dugin's geopolitics:

> With the accession of Putin, the search for a new national idea became more focused. But post-Soviet Russian society was not in a condition to base itself on the values that Communism had destroyed. Instead, the new attempts at a national idea bore an eerie resemblance to the Marxism-Leninism that Russians had so recently left behind.
>
> One such attempt was the theory of "Eurasianism," which posited a mortal opposition between a united Eurasia and a transatlantic West. ...
>
> According to the Eurasist platform, Eurasists and Atlantists "defend two different, alternative, mutually excluding images of the world and its future. It is the opposition between the Eurasists and Atlantists which defines the historical outline of the twenty-first century."[134]

David Satter decribes Dugin as "The most prominent exponent of this theory,"[135] but it would be more accurate to describe Dugin as the originator of this particular version of the Eurasianist doctrine, and it was a doctrine which found eager acceptance in those circles of Russia which found the greatest need for an external threat to provide an organizational principle for the State:

> In 1998 Dugin became an adviser to the speaker of the State Duma, Gennady Seleznyev, and in 1999 he became chairman of the geopolitical section of the Duma's Advisory Council on National Security. Nikolai Klokotov, the head of the Russian general staff,

---

134   David Satter, *It Was a Long Time Ago, and It Never Happened Anyway,* (New Haven and London: Yale University Press, 2012) p. 102–103.

135   ibid., p. 102.

wrote the preface for Dugin's book, and Colonel General Leonid Ivashov, a former high-ranking defense official, served as consultant. "In Russia it so happened," wrote the journalist Nikita Kaledin, that "the first people to feel the need of a national idea were the members of the defense industry. For them, it was necessary urgently to find an enemy in order to unite, rearm, and expand. ... Their imperial ideas coincided precisely with Dugin's Eurasian ideas."[136]

Following Dugin's departure from the *Pamyat'* movement, he began a period of interaction with the Communist Party of the Russian Federation, and although he soon went on to help establish the National Bolshevik Party (as detailed above), his views apparently had a lasting influence on the ideology of the chairman of the CPRF, Gennady Zyuganov. This influence on the CPRF has remained to this day. So, too, Dugin's influence on Vladimir Zhironovsky is palpably present in his rantings about the future exploits of the Russian military (a point which we will explore below).

Edmund Burke (1729–1797) referred to the ideology of the French Jacobins of his age as an "armed doctrine"— and such status as "armed doctrine" has been the character of ideology to this day. Dr. Russell Kirk (1918–1994) helpfully expanded on Burke's definition of ideology as follows:

> "Ideology" does not mean political theory or principle, even though many journalists and some professors commonly employ the term in that sense. Ideology really means political fanaticism—and, more precisely, the belief that this world of ours may be converted into the Terrestrial Paradise through the operation of positive law and positive planning. The ideologue—Communist or Nazi or of whatever affili-

---

136   ibid., p. 103.

ation—maintains that human nature and society may be perfected by mundane, secular means, though these means ordinarily involve social revolution. The ideologue immanentizes religious symbols and inverts religious doctrines.

What religion promises to the believer in a realm beyond time and space, ideology promises to everyone—except those who have been "liquidated" in the process—in society. Salvation becomes collective and political.[137]

Eurasianism is precisely such an "armed doctrine"—it is a form of Traditionalism inextricably bound up with an Evolan emphasis on the reform of society leading to the reform of man. It is Traditionalism on the march. In the words of Aleksandr Dugin:

Eurasianism implies a positive re-evaluation of the archaic, of the ancient. It fervently refers to the past, to the world of Tradition. The development of cultural process is seen by Eurasism in a new reference to the archaic, to the insertion of original cultural motives in the fabric of modern forms. The priority in this area is given back to national motives, to the sources of national creativity, to the continuation and revival of traditions.[138]

Laruelle recognizes that Dugin's Traditionalism and Eurasianism are bound together, claiming, "Dugin 'distorts' the idea of Eurasia by combining it with elements borrowed

---

137   "The Drug of Ideology" reprinted in Russell Kirk, *The Essential Russell Kirk,* ed. by George A. Panichas, (Wilmington, Delaware: ISI Books, 2007) p. 348–349.

138   "Eurasia above all—Manifest [sic] of the Eurasist movement" http://rossia3.ru/eng/Eurasiaabove [Accessed April 18, 2014]

from other intellectual traditions, such as theories of conservative revolution, the German geopolitics of the 1920s and 1930s, René Guénon's Traditionalism and the Western New Right."[139] But each of these influences which Laruelle enumerates are *all* related to, or influenced by, varying strains of occultism and Traditionalism—the fruits of Dugin's time in the Golovin circle are manifest in his Eurasianist notions. Traditionalism lent its influence, in varying degrees, to each of these 'elements.'

It has become common to refer to Dugin's ideology as "neo-Eurasianism" because of the differences between his vision of Eurasianism and that which was set forth in the 1920s. (However, it is worth noting that even those scholars who seem most adamant on the "new" character of Dugin's Eurasianism will often succumb to simply calling it "Eurasianism.") Though Eurasianism was probably largely forgotten in the West during the Soviet years, nonetheless it is certainly true that throughout the decade of the 1920s, the original form of Eurasianism was "the dominant ideological movement" within the Russian emigré community.[140] Just as Dugin is far from hostile toward Russia's Soviet past, the original Eurasians varied greatly with regard to their disagreement with the Bolsheviks; they resented being outside the policy-making structure of the new regime, and saw Bolshevism as a means by which the old Russian empire could expand: "The Eurasianists saw the continuation and expansion of the Russian Empire as an end in and of itself and justified such a position mainly through the unique geographical location and

---

139   Laruelle, *Aleksandr Dugin: A Russian Version of the European Radical Right?*, p. 5.

140   Steven K. Voytek, "Eurasianist Trends in Russian Foreign Policy: A Critical Analysis," (M.A. thesis, West Virginia University, 2012) p. 11. Also see Laruelle, *Russian Eurasianism—An Ideology of Empire*, p. 16–49.

80

ethnic composition of Russia."[141] When Dugin does not view the Eurasian empire as one which is simply (or exclusively) Russian, he is simply reiterating the teachings of the original Eurasianists:

> Paradoxically, "The Eurasians tried to preserve the Russian empire by denying its existence. There was no Russian empire, no Russia, only Eurasia, a harmonious, symphonic, organic association of peoples. ..." ... Establishing a discernable 'Eurasian' identity was therefore of crucial importance to classical Eurasianists.
>
> It is because of this that Eurasianists make the claim that Russia is neither Slavic nor Asian, but in fact a mixture of the two because of this long period of Mongol influence.[142]

However, Dugin's ideology is far more expansive in its territorial claims than was the original Eurasianism, and its claims vis-à-vis the historical character of the global struggle are vastly wider in scope. Traditionalism's syncretistic teachings places the emphasis on the coexistence of all those 'traditions' which purportedly descend from the 'Primordial Tradition' to be permissible within Eurasia, while 'parodies' such as "Protestanism" are excluded:

> Pronounced orientation toward the unification of Orthodoxy and Islam is a distinguishing feature of Neo-Eurasianism. Here Neo-Eurasiansists [sic] are much more radical than the founders of the ideology. ... Dugin accuses the first Eurasians of some residual Orthodox arrogance because they thought of Islam as of something like underdeveloped Orthodoxy. He writes that "the Orthodox Church and traditional

141   Voytek, p. 12–13.
142   ibid., p. 13–14.

(Shi'a, Hanafi, Sufi, in one word – Eurasian) Islam are full-fledged and genuine Eastern traditions, while Protestantism and the Wahhabist heresy are parodies, substitutes, resulting from the apocalyptic distortion of pure spirituality." The idea is that all "traditional" religions easily coexist, while their "profane," degraded versions conflict.

According to Dugin, tradition is a primeval and true world outlook that has been transformed and distorted throughout history. All worldviews based on tradition are religious and never put human beings at the center of the Universe. Dugin thereby does not talk about the conflict between Orthodoxy, Islam or Buddhism, for instance, or about "the clash of civilization" in the Huntingtonian sense. Instead, he focuses on conflict between various deviations from tradition. The West is the only civilization which has not descended from "real" tradition, and that is why all traditional religions should unite against it.[143]

Thus, again, one sees that no rapprochement with the West is possible: *only* the West is not descended from "real" tradition, therefore, all the rest of the world is inherently in conflict with the West, because "Civilizations are cultural and religious communities—not ethnic-national ones."[144]

Eurasianism is also not a recent expression of Dugin's thought; rather, it is simply an aspect of his overall worldview which has assumed a greater prominence as his ideology has moved nearer to becoming accepted by the Russian mainstream. Eurasianist ideas had already surfaced in the 1980s within *Pamyat'*, and Dugin was already promoting Eurasianism while serving

---

143   Mitrofanova, p. 53.
144   Dugin, *The Fourth Political Theory*, p. 165.

on the editorial board of *Den*'.[145] Dugin's belief in "Arctogaia" factors into his imaginary history of the struggle between Eurasianists and those whom he terms "Atlanticists," with "Arctogaia" a synonym for the Greek mythical land of Hyperborea[146]—a rather dramatic shift from the quaint Eurasianism of the 1920s:

> [Dugin] thus writes not merely about certain contradictions between Western civilization and "Eurasia" as, for instance, Kurginyan does. Instead, he draws the picture of an ancient conflict between Atlanticist Sea powers ("thallocracies"), going back to the sunken world of Atlantis and now headed by the "mondialist" United States, on the one side, and the Eurasian land powers ("tellurocracies"), originating with the mythic country of "Hyperborea" and now having as its most important component Russia, on the other. According to Dugin, the secret orders of these two antagonistic civilizations have been in an age-old struggle that is now entering its final stage.[147]

It must be understood that when Dugin is endeavoring to portray his Eurasianism in terms which relate it more closely to the real world, a mythical, dualistic battle between the children of Hyperborea and Atlantis is still the source of his thought, as we have already seen in his comments in the "Arctogaia Manifesto." That Dugin would hold to such fantasies is understandable, given his background as a Traditionalist: both René Guénon and Julius Evola also believed that such places had an actual, historical existence. Guénon cautions:

145   Laruelle, *Russian Eurasianism—An Ideology of Empire*, p. 5.

146   It is worth noting that the first journal published by Dugin's *Arctogaia* was *Giperboreyets* [*Hyperborean*] and Dugin wrote two books on the teachings of pertaining to Hyperborea and Ariosophy: *The Hyperborean Theory: An Ariosophical Investigation* (1993) and *Crusade of the Sun* (1996). Shenfield, p. 193.

147   Umland, "Toward an Uncivil Society?," p. 33.

One cannot be overprudent when it comes to civilizations that have entirely disappeared, and it is certainly not the attempts at reconstitution to which profane archeologists devote themselves that are likely to shed light on the question; but it is nonetheless true that many vestiges of a forgotten past are coming out of the earth in our age, and perhaps not without reason.[148]

However, such 'prudence' did not stop Guénon from speculating at length regarding the relative antiquity of the two civilizations and their relative geographical locations. For Guénon, Hyperborea is linked to "the primordial tradition, which was originally 'polar' in the literal sense of the word and whose starting-point is the very same as the present *Manvantara*, and the derivative and secondary Atlantean tradition, which relates to a much more restricted period."[149] Guénon comments on the historical impact of the Atlanteans on Toltec civilization as proof of the Western character of Atlantis, and of Atlantis being a mere "emanation from that of the Hyperborean *Tula*": "The very position of the Atlantean center on the East-West axis indicates its subordination with respect to the Hyperborean center, located at the North-South polar axis."[150]

Evola also refers to the Atlantean civilization as one which follows after the Hyperborean: "... the freezing and the long night descended at a specific time on the polar region. Thus, when the forced migration from the seat ensued, the first cycle came to an end and a new cycle—the Atlantic cycle—began."[151] The existence of these civilizations is not

148   René Guénon, *Traditional Forms & Cosmic Cycles*, trans. by Henry D. Fohr, (Hillsdale, New York: Sophia Perennis, 2003) p. 26.
149   ibid., p. 23.
150   ibid., p. 24.
151   Julius Evola, *Revolt Against the Modern World*, trans. by Guido Stucco, (Rochester, Vermont: Inner Traditions International, 1995) p. 189.

merely symbolic: Evola uses Hyperborea and Atlantis as a means to explain the historic origins of nations, and of 'Cro-Magnon' man:

> As far as the migration of the Northern primordial race is concerned, it is necessary to distinguish two great waves, the first moving from north to south, the second from west to east. Groups of Hyperboreans carrying the same spirit, the same blood, the same body of symbols, signs, and languages first reached North America and the northern regions of the Eurasian continent. Supposedly, tens of thousands of years later a second great migratory wave ventured as far as Central America, reaching a land situated in the Atlantic region that is now lost, thereby establishing a new center modeled after the polar regions. ...
>
> From this Atlantic seat the races of the second cycle spread to the American (hence the previously mentioned memories of the Nahuatlans, Toltecs, and Aztecs concerning their original homeland), European, and African continents. ... Anthropologically speaking, these races correspond to Cro-Magnon man, who made his appearance toward the end of the glacial age in the western Part of Europe (especially in the area of the French Cantabric civilization of Abri La Madeleine, Gourdain, and Altamira); Cro-Magnon man was clearly superior, both culturally and biologically, to the aboriginal Mousterian man of the Ice Age, so much so that somebody recently nicknamed the Cro-Magnon "the Greeks of the Paleolithic." As far as their origin is concerned, the similarity between their civilization and the civilization of the Hyperborean, which is found even in the vestiges of the people of the Far North (civilization of the reindeer), is very significant.[152]

152   Evola, p. 195–6.

Given his delusions regarding the origins of the peoples of the earth, one gets the context for Evola's concern that "one can say that the superior Western races have been agonizing for many centuries and that the increasing growth in world population has the same meaning as the swarming of worms on a decomposing organism or as the spreading of cancerous cells".[153]

Dugin's adherence to a Hyperborean theory which seems related to that of Lanz has been noticed by scholars over the years. Thus Shenfield wrote in 2001:

> Dugin counterposes not only an "Eastern" (Eurasian) to a "Western" (Atlantic) civilizational heritage, but also a "Northern" to a "Southern" tradition. He believes that in the distant past there was an island paradise in the Arctic north called Hyperborea that was home to a pure Aryan or Hyperborean race, the ancestors of today's Russians. The Hyperboreans were in touch with a transcendent spiritual reality. Later they migrated south through Eurasia, where they established great civilizations but also lost their original racial purity and spiritual powers. The Aryans are set against the more primitive and earthbound dark-skinned people of the tropical south (Dugin 1996a). These ideas are taken from the mystical racist doctrine of Ariosophy that appeared in Germany and Austria at the end of the nineteenth century and was one of the precursors of Nazism (Goodricke-Clarke 1992).[154]

As noted earlier, Dugin subscribes to a form of geopolitical thinking which is expressed in terms of "sacred geography." Thus, the discussion of the "North-South axis"

153   ibid., p. 167.
154   Stephen Shenfield, *Russian Fascism—Traditions, Tendencies, Movements,* (2001) p. 196–197.

and its primacy over the "East-West axis" is reflected in Dugin's writings in a way which is reflective of his Traditionalist beliefs, and forms a central Traditionalist aspect of his Eurasianist ideology. In his essay, "From Sacred Geography to Geopolitics,"[155] Dugin maintains that "geopolitics stands in an intermediate place between traditional science (sacred geography) and profane science." Thus, one may presume that Dugin will alternate between the mystical language of "sacred geography" preserved for his fellow Traditionalists, while retaining the ability to express his ideology in the mundane "desacralized" terminology of geopolitics. In "From Sacred Geography to Geopolitics," Dugin makes it clear that he wholeheartedly subscribes to a Traditionalist interpretation of the world in which geopolitical realities have mystical meanings (e.g., "No empire has its centre in mountain regions. Hence the so often repeated motive of sacred geography: 'mountains are populated by demons'."). Dugin is careful to remove the racist content of much of the early twentieth century discussion of the "North-South axis," but his loathing for the West appears to be something he cannot bring himself to disassociate from the most prominent nation of the West:

> The West has the opposite symbolic meaning. It is the "country of death", the "lifeless word", the "green country" (as the ancient Egyptians called it). West is "the empire of exile", "the pit of the rejected", according to the expression of Islamic mystics. ...
> Along the East-West axis were drawn peoples and civilizations, possessing hierarchical characters—closer to the East were those closer to Sacral, to Tradition, to spiritual wealth. Closer to West, those of a more decayed, degraded and dying Spirit. ...
> The West is the centre of "material" and "technological" development. At the cultural-ideological level,

---

155   available at http://evrasia.info/article/416 [Accessed May 19, 2014]

there "liberal-democratic" tendencies, individualistic and humanist world views are prevailing. ... Gradually a peculiar "Western ideology" was cast in the universal formula of "ideology of human rights", which became a dominant principle in the most western regions of the planet—Northern America, and first of all the US.

However, while Dugin identifies the West with "the West," he reverses the image when it comes to the sacred North. Those people who are either of "the North" (spiritual) or of "the South" (materialist) are mixed together: "... the typological dualism of the 'people of the North' and the 'people of the South' was preserved in all times and epochs—but not as much as an external conflict of two miscellaneous civilizations, as an internal conflict within the framework of the same civilization." "North" (the spiritual inclination) does not mean North (the direction) because Hyperborea no longer exists:

Firstly, the paleocontinent of North, Hyperborea, since many millennia already does not exist on a physical level, remaining a spiritual reality, on which is directed the spiritual look of the initiated, exacting the original Tradition.

Secondly, the ancient nordic race, the race of the "white teachers", coupled with the pole in the primordial epoch, does not coincide at all with what is commonly agreed to call today the "white race", based only on physical characters [sic], on the colour of the skin, etc. ...

Thus, North in Tradition is a meta-historical and meta-geographical reality. The same can be said also about the "hyperborean race"—a "race" not in the biological, but in a pure spiritual, metaphysical sense.

Or, one might say, a Gnostic sense: Dugin's "Hyperboreans" are the "initiated" (his term) who wage war against "the West"—just as one may observe in his "Arctogaia Manifesto." But when Dugin is *not* referring to Arctogaia and a mystical warfare, how does he dress Traditionalist Eurasianism in terms comprehensible to mere mortals? Let us turn, once again, to his "Main Principles of Eurasist Policy."[156] After Dugin made the three-fold distinction of "reciprocally conflicting patterns of state strategy" which we examined above, he turned to a more extensive examination of the foreign and domestic policy of Eurasianism.

A recurrent theme of Dugin's foreign policy is his stated preference for a multipolar world, contrary to a presumed unipolar world which he posits that the United States/"New World Order" is attempting to establish. Dugin will often rail against 'the hegemony of mondialism' (or words to that effect) by which he means to refer to the conspiratorial notion that there are forces at work which are trying to suppress all civilizations in favor of the one civilization—that of Western globalization—which is trying to eliminate all meaningful forms of national or local government in order to impose Western civilization on the entire world.

To confront the threat of a unipolar world, Dugin proposes that Russia rank the nations of the world in terms of their potential relationship to Eurasia:

> The first category: powerful regional formations (countries or groups of countries), whose relations with Russia can be conveniently expressed by the term "complementary." It means that the countries own something vital for Russia, while Russia owns something extremely indispensable for them. ...

156   "Main Principles of Eurasist Policy," www.4pt.su.k0.gfns.net/tr/node/30 [Accessed April 18, 2014]

The second category: geopolitical formations being interested in multipolarity, but not being symmetrically complementary to Russia. ...

The third category represents the countries of the Third World which do not possess enough geopolitical potential to claim even the status of limited subjects. ...

The fourth category: the US and the countries of the American continent laying [sic] under US control.

Dugin places the European Union, Japan, Iran, and India within the first category, looking for "economic and technological sponsorship" from the EU and Japan and "political-strategic partnership in the South" from Iran and India. (It should be noted that in recent years Dugin may be inclined to include Turkey in such a category of "political-strategic partnership"—especially as the cultural division between Turkey and the nations of the European Union continues to grow.[157]) What Dugin proposes to provide such "first category" powers is that which the past century has taught the world to expect from Russia: "resources, strategic potential of weapons, political weight."

Dugin's "second category" includes China, Pakistan, and the Arab countries. These are nations which Dugin proposes must be neutralized, lest they align with the United States: they must not be included within "the eurasist project," but they must also be alienated from supporting the West: "With regard to the countries of this category Russia must act with the utmost caution - not including them in the eurasist project, but at the same time aiming at neutralising as much as possible the negative potential of their reaction

---

157   see Marlène Laruelle, *Russo-Turkish Rapprochement through the Idea of Eurasia: Alexander Dugin's Networks in Turkey*, (Washington, D.C.: The Jamestown Foundation, 2008).

and actively countering their active inclusion in the process of unipolar globalisation..."

The "third category" consists of "Third World" nations which (it appears to this reader) Dugin intends to 'divvy up' among the zones of the "first category" powers: "Concerning these countries Russia should follow differentiated policies, contributing to their political integration in zones of 'common prosperity', under the control of the mighty partners of Russia within the Eurasian bloc." And Dugin does not hesitate to offer specifics regarding which "mighty partners" should gain the spoils of his war with the West: "This means that in the Pacific zone it is convenient for Russia to favor the strengthening of the Japanese presence. In Asia it is necessary to encourage the geopolitical ambitions of India and Iran. It is also necessary to contribute to expanding the European Union influence in the Arab world and Africa as a whole." One may well wonder how the inhabitants of such regions and nations would react to the notion that behind Putin's and Dugin's blustering against 'American hegemony' rests a plan to resuscitate the failed imperial ambitions of Japan and several European nations. What is certain is that the exercise of such ambitions will certainly create a demand for the Russian weapons which Dugin proposes providing to "first category" powers, because his plan for nations of the "third category" could easily mean a century of war which would outstrip the horrors of the twentieth century.

As for the nations of the "fourth category"—"the US and countries of the American continent laying [sic] under US control"—Dugin also promises more warfare:

> Rigidly and actively using to this purpose, first of all, the instrument of the Eurasian alliance, opposing such globalisation, Russia should on the contrary support the isolationist tendency in the US, saluting with favour the limitation of US geopolitical interests to

the American continent. ... And if unipolar globalisation will keep being staged, it is Russia's interest to
back the anti-American mood in Southern and Central
America, using, however, a much more flexible and
wider world-view and geopolitical device than Marxism. In the same channel lays [sic] the policy of priority work with anti-American political circles in Canada
and Mexico. Possibly also using in this direction the
lobbyist activity of the Eurasian diasporas in the US.

For those readers who remember the type of chaos which
Soviet weapons and treachery worked in Central and South
America, it will be immediately recognized that Dugin is not
issuing an empty threat. Nor should it be imagined that his
invocation of "lobbyist activity of the Eurasian diasporas" is
anything less than what the people of the world have seen as
such 'lobbyist activities' in recent months in Ukraine, where
Russian thugs—armed with Russian weapons and assisted
by the 'little green men' of the Russian special forces—have
brought chaos and death to a peaceful nation which had the
temerity to oppose Putin's plans for Eurasia.

In his "Main Principles...," one gets a sense of the future of the nations which have been subjugated to the Eurasian empire. Dugin begins to describe his "domestic policy"
with the declaration:

"The integration of CIS countries into a united Eurasian
Union is the major strategic imperative of eurasism."

The meaning of these words should be taken quite literally.
The CIS—Commonwealth of Independent States—came into
being after the collapse of the Soviet Union. It includes Russia, Armenia, Azerbaijan, Belarus, Kazakhstan, Kyrgyzstan,
Moldova, Tajikistan, and Uzbekistan. Turkmenistan is an
unofficial, associate member. Georgia, although it was once

a member, has understandably withdrawn from the CIS after contending with naked, Russian military aggression. Ukraine's already tenuous connection to the CIS moved toward an open breach when Russia illegally seized Crimea.[158] By Dugin declaring that the integration of *all* of these states into the Eurasian Union is a "strategic imperative" one can readily see why the Putin regime is unwilling to stop its aggression toward Ukraine: the Eurasian Union is meaningless without it.

As regards the political system of the Eurasian Union, Dugin declares in the "Main Principles..." that "The Supreme Leader of the Eurasian Union must concentrate the common will to the achievement of power and prosperity of the state"—language which seems quite reminiscent of claims made in the 1940s regarding the unification of *"ein volk."* Although Dugin speaks of the rights of the 'peoples' and 'ethnoses' of Eurasia, he makes it clear that there will most certainly not be the freedoms which the peoples of the West take for granted: "The qualitative understanding of the social factor allows precisely to define the golden mean between the hyper-individualism of bourgeois West and the hyper-collectivism of socialist East." For Dugin, freedom and slavery appear to be extremes to be avoided for the sake of 'a golden mean'. (Serfdom, for example, would rest between these extremes. It should also be noted that when the *quality* of one's rights is stressed—and not the *quantity*—it can be taken for granted that the *quantity* will be reduced.) Furthermore, the state will be the arbiter of morality:

> The Eurasian society should be founded on the principle of a revived moral possessing both common features and concrete forms **linked to the specificity of the ethno-confessional context**. The principles of

158   http://www.kyivpost.com/content/politics/bill-introduced-to-withdraw-ukraine-from-cis-339433.html [Accessed May 13 2014]

naturalness, purity, restraint, respect for the rules, liability, healthy life, righteousness and truthfulness are common to **all traditional faiths** of Eurasia. These undeniable moral values must be given the status of state norms. Scandalous vices, impudent and public violation of moral foundations should be ruthlessly rooted out. [emphasis added]

Under such a notion of law, there is no difference between what a culture deems to be "immoral" and what the state declares to be "illegal." What is all the more intriguing is that Dugin links the state imposition of such standards to the various specific contexts of different ethno-cultural groups. "Eurasist federalism" means that the various nations which enter the Eurasian Union "will forever liquidate," with a "compensation" for "the peoples of the Eurasian Union" receiving "the possibility of maximal development of ethnic, religious and even, in some definite issues, juridical independence." Among other implications of such ethno-cultural notions of the rule of law is that while Muslim nations will lose their national identity within the Union, "juridical independence" may exist, according to their "ethno-confessional context." Presumably, for example, this would mean that Muslims could be held accountable to *sharia* courts, in accordance with the standards of their community; thus, those things that are deemed "scandalous vices" could be "ruthlessly rooted out." At the heart of Dugin's notion of "rights" is the observation: "The undoubted strategic unity in eurasist federalism is accompanied by ethnic plurality, by the emphasis on the juridical element of the 'rights of the peoples.'" Note: not the rights of *people* (i.e., the legal rights of individuals), but the rights of *peoples* (i.e., *groups*).

The farce which Eurasianism makes of the rule of law extends into other areas, as well. Thus we are told that "loyalty to the eurasist idea" will be one of the criteria for the field of education (which would, presumably, make state propaganda a primary function of education) while the "principle of freedom of speech must be combined with the imperative of liability for the freely spoken words." In a nation with a brutal history of imposing liabilities on 'freely spoken words' in the past—a society where such liabilities could include imprisonment in the Soviet Gulag or in a psychiatric prison—can one reasonably imagine a meaningful right to dissent from the Eurasianist ideology in Dugin's imagined union—when the outcome of the ancient war between Hyperborea and Atlantis is at stake?

As noted previously, Dugin's Eurasianism claims a much more expansive role for itself than any previous form of the ideology, and it claims for itself a universality which cannot theoretically exceed the claims of Marxism-Leninism (which, after all, had decreed that it would ultimately triumph over the entire human race), but which, practically-speaking, already marks out on the map for itself an empire with much more generous borders than has been seen previously.

Unlike the Eurasianists of the 1920s, Dugin does not talk of an irreducible and romantic opposition between East and West; in Dugin's theories, both Asia and Europe are destined to come under Russian-Eurasian domination.

As the maritime and democratic enemy allegedly has a "fifth column" in Russia, Dugin calls for a restoration of the Soviet Union and a reorganization of the Russian Federation. He is the only Neo-Eurasianist to include in his political project not only the Baltic States, but the whole former socialist bloc. His Eurasia must even expand beyond Soviet space, as he proposes to incorporate Manchuria, Xingjian, Tibet, and Mongolia, as well as the Orthodox world of the Balkans: Eurasia would only reach its limits with "geopolitical expansion to the shores of the Indian ocean," an idea that was taken up and popularized by Zhirinovskii.[159]

Indeed, Vladimir Zhirinovsky's infamous "Last Bid for the South" was, for a brief time, a cause for alarm in the West during the mid-1990s. Zhirinovsky sudden prominence in Russian politics in the aftermath of the collapse of the Soviet Union was, perhaps, a harbinger of things to come. Zhirinovsky's absurdly misnamed "Liberal-Democratic Party" gave the appearance of having 'come from nowhere' when he received over six million votes in the first presidential elections after the collapse of the Soviet regime. When setting forth his Eurasian vision, Zhirinovsky's tone lacks refinement, but his agenda was befitting of Dugin's apocalyptic self-importance:

The Indian Ocean that now washes India's shores will one day lap at Russia's southernmost extremity. Indeed, Russia's borders that once abutted the city of Kushka, in southern Turkmenia, will run through one of the Indian Ocean's new ports, with connecting railways to Delhi, Teheran, and Baghdad. ... To save themselves, Russians should descend southward. No one will change our mind or stop us. No one.

America—the only country that could oppose us—will step back, for it holds its own fate dear. And unlike Afghanistan, Iran, and Turkey, it will not lose its ability to live. Russia has nothing to lose. We will go down to the South as liberators, to put a stop to violence. We will go where people, surrounded by blood, wake up and go to sleep to the sound of bullets and explosions, where they live amid violence and looting. Russian soldiers will stop this butchery, this violence, this outrage to human culture. And Russian soldiers

159   Laruelle, *Aleksandr Dugin: A Russian Version of the European Radical Right?*, p. 7.

will themselves come to a stop on the shore of the warm Indian Ocean, establishing there new outposts, settlements, resorts, and sentries. With floodlights, Russian soldiers will illuminate the frontier waters of the Indian Ocean.[160]

In a sense, it is almost unfortunate that Zhironovsky's Eurasianism drew premature interest from the West: by linking the doctrine to his absurd personage, interest in the ideology died away almost as quickly as his political fortunes. Now, Dugin's Eurasianism is dangerously close to becoming the overt policy of the Putin regime. With the establishment of his Eurasian Youth Union in 2004, the ideology gained a new tool to reach the disaffected and dispirited young people of the former Soviet Union—and beyond. With 47 offices through Russia and nine offices abroad, the Eurasian Youth Union has vastly extended the reach of Dugin's doctrines.

Dugin has also personally received the institutional credibility for which a counter-culture academic yearns: appointment to a position at the most credible educational institution in Russia—Moscow State University—and a high profile role in the Russian media.[161] As for Putin, his plan to establish the Eurasian Union was proclaimed to the world in November 2011. But the West may relax, for he has declared that "... none of this entails any kind of revival of the Soviet Union. It would be naïve to try to revive or emulate something that has been consigned to history."[162] ("Naïve," mind

160   Vladimir Zhirinovsky, *My Struggle,* (New York: Barricade Books, 1996) p. 64, 67–8.

161   "His outsized presence in Russian public life is a sign of Putin's approval; Russian media, particularly television, is controlled almost entirely by the Kremlin." Barbashin and Thoburn, *Putin's Brain—Alexander Dugin and the Philosophy Behind Putin's Invasion of Crimea.*

162   http://www.russianmission.eu/en/news/article-prime-minister-vladimir-putin-new-integration-project-eurasia-future-making-

you—not "criminal" or "barbaric.")

Oh, and he won't annex Crimea, either.

What seems certain is that whatever doubts Dugin might have had concerning Putin over the years, he is now adamant in his support for 'the leader.' During a September 2008 interview for the Los Angeles Times[163], Dugin was confronted with the observation, "Your views on Vladimir Putin have fluctuated." Dugin replied:

> I appreciated very much his concrete steps to reinforce political order in Russia, his steps to get away the oligarchs, to diminish influence of Westerners and to save Russian territorial unity in the Chechnya situation.
>
> But also I saw that he was encircled by pro-Western, pro-liberal politicians and advisors and experts ... and that was main reason for my criticism toward him.
>
> But I think that now, after [Russia's military intervention in Georgia on] Aug. 8, Putin and Medvedev have passed the irreversible point. They have shown that the will and the decision to put the words into practice are in fact irreversible. So my support to Putin and Medvedev is now absolute.
>
> I was deceived by these circles. But at the same time, maybe the West also was deceived by them.

izvestia-3- [Accessed May 13, 2014]

163   Megan Stack, "Russian nationalist advocates Eurasian alliance against the U.S." September 4, 2008. www.latimes.com/world/la-fgw-dugin4-2008sep4-story.html [Accessed May 9, 2014]

Dugin's Eurasianism and the Birth of a Gnostic Mass Movement

The meaning of Russia is that through the Russian people will be realized the last thought of God, the thought of the End of the World. ... Death is the way to immortality. Love will begin when the world ends. ... We are uprooting the accursed Tree of Knowledge. With it will perish the Universe.[164]

In 1968, Political philosopher Eric Voegelin established a term—the *gnostic mass movement*—which has proven to be of remarkable hermeneutical value for those who seek to understand the character of various ideologies of the Modern ages. Voegelin acknowledged that although such movements have exerted a great deal of influence throughout the course of events in recent generations, nonetheless it remains quite difficult to define the unifying character of such movements.

Gnosticism is usually defined by a fundamental pessimism about the world; Gnostics have also been marked by their elitist propensities and initiatory character. This means that most of the ancient Gnostics had very little interest in 'winning over' the masses; in fact, the exclusive character of their *gnosis*—'knowledge'—was seen as proof that they were 'special.' Only by being initiated into the 'mysteries' of a particular Gnostic sect could one become 'one who knows.' Their elitism led the Gnostics to hold Christians in contempt, because Christ's teachings were available for all to learn. As Jesus declared in John 18:20: "I spoke openly to the world. I always taught in synagogues and in the temple, where the Jews always meet, and in secret I have said nothing." Gnosticism appeals to the fallen human desire for a secret knowledge;

---

164   Dugin quoted by Shenfield, p. 197.

Christians look at that desire as one which is recognizable as the greed for hidden 'wisdom' which led Eve into sin (Gen. 3:6).

From groups such as the Valentinians of late antiquity (ca. second century A.D.), to medieval heretical movements such as the Cathars (twelfth to fourteenth centuries A.D.), Gnostic movements have characteristically rejected the world as a place which is irredeemably evil—a place created by an evil demiurge and which must be escaped—and the adherents of such Gnostic movements have shown contempt for those who are not privy to their 'secret' insights into the fundamental order of the universe, even as they have required participation in initiatory rituals to gain admittance to their ranks.

As noted previously, the pessimistic character of Gnostic movements was significantly abated by the influence of Hermetic doctrines which, given their common association with belief in alchemy, see the world as marked by evil, but also as a place which can be *transformed*. Renaissance-era Hermetic 'reformers'—men such as Marsilio Ficino (1433–1499) and Giovanni Pico della Mirandola (1463–1494)—retained the elitism of Gnosticism, but moved their doctrines into the light of day by publishing them. Thus, many of the groups which Voegelin identifies as "gnostic mass movements" are heirs, at least in part, to the Hermetic Reformation of the fifteenth and sixteenth centuries. In its initial phase, the Hermetic Reformation remained primarily within the elite ranks of the *intelligentsia*; its initiates were found among the ranks of the scholars of the Renaissance. Because of their elite character, such intellectual movements had a more limited direct influence on society. When the Gnostic movements gained a 'mass' character—that is, ceased to be 'elite'—they also immediately became more diffuse in their influence.

According to Voegelin, the "gnostic mass movements" have shaped the course of the modern age. As Voegelin explained in *Science, Politics and Gnosticism:*

By gnostic movements we mean such movements as progressivism, positivism, Marxism, psychoanalysis, communism, fascism, and national socialism. We are not dealing, therefore, in all of these cases with political mass movements. ... None of the movements cited began as a mass movement; all derived from intellectuals and small groups.[165]

Thus, a "gnostic mass movement" begins from a small circle; it is precisely the capacity for a particular body of Gnostic doctrine to be comprehensible (at least in terms of its broad outline) and accepted by a more popular audience that transforms a Gnostic elite circle into a "gnostic mass movement." Such mass movements are inherently Hermetic in character: they are aimed at reform of the world—they are politicized doctrines which may keep the trappings of Christian terminology, while fundamentally subverting the doctrinal content of the terms. The "gnostic mass movements" teach and act upon "armed doctrines"—their adherents pursue particular paths of perfectionism which are meant to be accomplished in this life (thus their goals are "immanentized"), even though the fulfillment of that path would mean a version of an "end of history" (thus, they are "eschatological" in character). Voegelin thus defines three different types of "gnostic mass movement" based on the particular characteristics of their immanentized eschatology:

The gnostic mass movements derive their ideas of perfection from the Christian. In accordance with the components just described, there are on principle three possibilities of derivation. In gnostic perfection, which is supposed to come to pass within the historical world, the teleological and axiological components

165   Eric Voegelin, *Science, Politics and Gnosticism*, (Wilmington, Delaware: ISI Books, 2004) p. 61–62.

can be immanentized either separately or together. ...

To the first type of derivation, the teleological, belongs progressivism in all variants. When the teleological component is immanentized, the chief emphasis of the gnostic-political idea lies on the forward movement, on the movement toward a goal of perfection. ...

In the second type of derivation, the axiological, the emphasis of the idea falls on the state of perfection in the world. Conditions for a perfect social order are described and worked out in detail and assume the form of an ideal image. Such an image was first sketched by Thomas More in his *Utopia*. ...

In the third type of derivation, the two components are immanentized together, and there is present both a conception of the end goal and knowledge of the methods by which it is to be brought about. We shall speak of cases of this third type as *activist mysticism*. Under activist mysticism belong primarily movements that descend from Auguste Comte and Karl Marx.[166]

It would be our contention that Dugin's fusion of Traditionalism and Eurasianism has become a "gnostic mass movement" of the third type, "activist mysticism." It is not an exaggeration to state that Dugin's intended goal, his *telos,* is the End of the World, and that the accomplishment of that end is dependent, he believes, on the implementation of his ideology. As Dugin has proclaimed in his recent book, *The Fourth Political Theory*:

The end times and the eschatological meaning of politics will not realize themselves on their own. We will wait for the end in vain. The end will never come if we wait for it, and it will never come if we do not. ... If

166   Voegelin, p. 66–68.

the Fourth Political Practice is not able to realise the end of times, then it would be invalid. The end of days should come, but it will not come by itself. This is a task, it is not a certainty. It is an active metaphysics. It is a practice.[167]

This desire to bring about the end of the world is not a sudden development in Dugin's thought. As noted in the quotation at the beginning of this chapter, as early as 2001, Dugin's intentions were being published abroad, and could be read by an English-speaking audience. In 2001, Shenfield observes that Dugin's eschatological view is 'Manichean'—which is to say, a dualistic form of Gnosticism which views the world as a battleground of equally matched forces of good and evil, in which spiritual forces of light contend with material forces of evil. Into this Manichaeism, Dugin admixes Christian concepts, oft repeating the notion that the West is the realm of 'Antichrist.' As Shenfield quotes Dugin:

The meaning of Russia is that through the Russian people will be realized the last thought of God, the thought of the End of the World. ... Death is the way to immortality. Love will begin when the world ends. We must long for it, like true Christians. ... We are uprooting the accursed Tree of Knowledge. With it will perish the Universe.[168]

Shenfield then observes: "Alexander Yanov, quoting these lines, concludes that Dugin's 'real dream is of death, first of all the death of Russia.' In his reply, Dugin avoids dealing directly with the substance of Yanov's critique, but observes that he fails to appreciate the positive significance of death..."[169]

167   Dugin *The Fourth Political Theory*, p. 183.
168   Dugin quoted by Shenfield, p. 197.
169   ibid.

It is hard to know how to react to someone who claims to want to bring about the end of the world. When that desire is expressed with a thick Russian accent, the hearer is all the more likely to simply dismiss the speaker as some sort of 'super villain' from a bad 'action/adventure' movie. It is a claim which evokes a snicker—until one realizes that the man who thinks that the "meaning of Russia" is "the End of the World" is the man whose geopolitical doctrine is being implemented by the ruler of Russia.

Traditionalism is not a teaching for idle hands: "Working on a long-term project of cultural and spiritual renewal, the Traditionalists seek to change hearts, minds, and spirits to undermine and ultimately defeat the thoroughly 'decadent' modern world."[170] For Dugin, as for Evola before him, Traditionalist belief is expressed in support for violent action. Thus Clowes cites Dugin's words from a 1998 interview: "If the European New Right chooses us [Russians], that means it chooses the barbarian element, and therefore it must choose our methods of action," [Dugin] says. He notes that the New World Order will not come about by means of "aging gentlemen meeting in seminars." He advises the following: "You must take a knife, put on a mask, go out of the house in the evening and kill at least one Yank." He adds, "I do not know whether any of the New Right activists have ever been under artillery siege, but our people do not only go to meetings or fight at the barricades, they also go to real wars, for instance to the Dniestr district [Moldova], or to Yugoslavia. ... The New Right is only a project, and we are its architects. The future truly is ours."[171]

---

170   Stéphane François, "The *Nouvelle Droite* and 'Tradition,'" in *Journal for the Study of Radicalism,* 8:1 (2004) p. 104.
171   Clowes, p. 43.

Americans are so used to seeing such rhetoric haunting the outer edges of the lunatic fringe that the inherent instinct is to dismiss such rhetoric—until one remembers the 53 protesters allegedly murdered by government snipers in the final days of the struggle to overthrow the corrupt regime of Viktor Yanukovych. The blood of the martyrs of Kiev flowed in the streets at a time when the Ukrainian people remember quite well that last year marked the eightieth anniversary of the *Holodomor*—the "extermination by hunger"—when the Soviet regime deliberately starved to death as many as seven million Ukrainians in a single year of planned famine.[172] As noted in the Introduction, the Ukrainian government has long understood the nature of Aleksandr Dugin's agenda: that's why he was declared years ago to be a *persona non grata* and was banned from entering into Ukraine. And they understand the implications of one of his followers being arrested in Kiev for allegedly seeking support for further acts of violence against the government and people of Ukraine. As for friendly relations between Ukraine and the United States, Dugin was asked in 2008, "How does Russia view the development of friendly relations between the United States and former Soviet republics such as Ukraine and Georgia?" He replied:

As a declaration of war. As a declaration of psychological, geopolitical, economic and open war.[173]

This is the fruit of Eurasianist ideology: a zero-sum global battleground. It is apparently irrelevant that Ukraine is an independent nation: an improvement in relations between

172   For an overview of the Ukrainian *Holodomor*, please see Miron Dolot, *Execution by Hunger—The Hidden Holocaust*, (New York and London: W. W. Norton & Co., 1985).
173   Megan Stack, "Russian nationalist advocates Eurasian alliance against the U.S." September 4, 2008. www.latimes.com/world/la-fgw-dugin4-2008sep4-story.html [Accessed May 9, 2014]

Ukraine and the Western world is interpreted as a declaration of war.

In the same interview, Dugin was asked: "If Ukraine were to move into NATO, what do you think the Russian reaction would be?" Dugin declared:

> I think that the Russian reaction would be to support an uprising in eastern parts and Crimea and I could not exclude the entrance of armed force there, as in the Ossetian scenario.
>
> But the difference is that half of the Ukrainian population is Russian,[174] is directly Russian, and this half of the population regards itself as being oppressed by the values, by the language, by the geopolitical issues, completely against their will. So I don't think that, in this case, direct intervention of Russian armed force will be needed. I think on the eve of entrance into NATO there will be public riots and the split of Ukraine into two parts.

The parallels between the strategy which Dugin set forth in 2008 and the events which are playing out in 2014 are uncanny. And however the events play out in the coming months for the people of Ukraine, Aleksandr Dugin is prepared to offer a Eurasianist interpretation of those events which will no doubt set it in the context of his twilight struggle at the End of the World.

But there are further hermeneutical insights to be derived from Voegelin's *Science, Politics and Gnosticism* which will help us to understand a "gnostic mass movement" such as Eurasianism. Voegelin observed:

> A second complex of symbols that runs through mod-

_____

174   Actually, official census statistics report only approximately 17 percent of the population of Ukraine is composed of ethnic Russians.

ern gnostic mass movements was created in the speculation on history of Joachim of Flora at the end of the twelfth century. ... He projected his view of history on a trinitarian scheme. World history was a consequence of three great ages—those of the Father, the Son, and the Holy Spirit.[175]

The present author has written rather extensively concerning the influence of Joachim of Fiore's (1135-1202) view of history over the past eight centuries.[176] However, for the purposes of briefly relating Dugin's Eurasianist ideology in terms of Joachimite speculation, a few points of comparison between Dugin's claims and Voegelin's description of Joachimism are worth noting.

Voegelin observed: "The first of these symbols is that of the Third Realm—that is, the conception of a third world-historical phase that is at the same time the last, the age of fulfillment. An extensive class of gnostic ideas come under the symbol of the three phases."[177]

Dugin is quite keen on the notion that the coming age is the third, and final, age. As Dugin wrote in "The metaphysics of national-bolshevism":[178]

Beyond "rights" and "lefts", there's one and indivisible Revolution, in the dialectical triad "third Rome - Third Reich - third International."

The realm of national-bolshevism, Regnum, their Empire of the End, this is the perfect accomplishment of the greatest Revolution of the history, both

175 Voegelin, p. 69.
176 The influence of Joachimite speculation is treated throughout *A Time for Every Purpose Under Heaven* (Malone, Texas: Repristination Press, 2012), but it receives particular focus in pp. 53–70, 139–180, and 273–290.
177 Voegelin, p. 70.
178 http://arctogaia.com/public/eng-teor.htm [Accessed May 9, 2014]

continental and universal one. It is the angels' return, heroes' resurrection, the heart's uprising against the reason's dictatorship. This last revolution is a concern of the acephal, the headless bearer of the cross, sickle and hammer, crowned by eternal sun fylfot.

This "Empire of the End" is marked by the "dialectical triad" which combines "Third Rome–Third Reich—Third International." All the expectations of historic Russian messianic delusions, combined with the Joachimite aims of Nazism and Soviet Bolshevism, purportedly find their highest expression in this new ideology, according to Dugin.

Voegelin further noted that, "And the new age, like the preceding ones, was to be ushered in by the appearance of a leader. As the first age began with Abraham and the second with Christ, so the third was to begin in the year 1260 with the appearance of a *dux e Babylone.*"[179] And: "The second symbol Joachim developed is that of the leader, the *dux*, who appears at the beginning of a new era and through his appearance establishes that era."[180]

In our assessment, Dugin has very clearly flagged the identity of his *dux e Babylone*: "Speaking to the Political Council of *Evraziia* in 2001 Dugin insisted that 'true Eurasianism can only be achieved via Putin. What stands against Putin is pseudo-Eurasianism.'"[181] Although his trust in Putin has wavered over the years, Dugin is now thoroughly committed to Putin as the man who can bring to pass his dreams of Eurasia:

> I appreciated very much his concrete steps to reinforce political order in Russia, his steps to get away the oligarchs, to diminish influence of Westerners and to save Russian territorial unity in the Chechnya situation.

---

179   Voegelin, p. 70.
180   ibid., p. 71.
181   Mitrofanova, p. 192.

But also I saw that he was encircled by pro-Western, pro-liberal politicians and advisors and experts ... and that was main reason for my criticism toward him.

But I think that now, after [Russia's military intervention in Georgia on] Aug. 8, Putin and Medvedev have passed the irreversible point. They have shown that the will and the decision to put the words into practice are in fact irreversible. So my support to Putin and Medvedev is now absolute.[182]

The rise of Eurasianism as an ideological force in Russia owes much to the favor which Putin has bestowed on Dugin since 2001. But the Eurasianist ideology may have grown to a proportion in which it now gives Dugin a profound level of influence over Putin:

Dugin's ideology has influenced a whole generation of conservative and radical activists and politicians, who, if given the chance, would fight to adopt its core principles as state policy. Considering the shabby state of Russian democracy, and the country's continued move away from Western ideas and ideals, one might argue that the chances of seeing neo-Eurasianism conquer new ground are increasing. Although Dugin's form of it is highly theoretical and deeply mystical, it is proving to be a strong contender for the role of Russia's chief ideology. Whether Putin can control it as he has controlled so many others is a question that may determine his longevity.[183]

182   Megan Stack, "Russian nationalist advocates Eurasian alliance against the U.S." September 4, 2008. www.latimes.com/world/la-fgw-dugin4-2008sep4-story.html [Accessed May 9, 2014]

183   Anton Barbashin and Hannah Thoburn, "Putin's Brain—Alexander Dugin and the Philosoph Behind Putin's Invasion of Crimea" (Dated March 31, 2014) www.foreignaffairs.com/articles/141080/alton-bar-

It will be seen whether or not Putin could (or would) retain power without Eurasianism. For the moment, his pursuit of the Eurasian Union makes it clear that he has no interest in abandoning Eurasianism (a point which we will pursue further in the next chapter). And it is precisely this influence of Eurasianism over "the Leader" which brings us to Voegelin's third Joachimite symbol:

> The third of Joachim's symbols is that of the prophet. Joachim assumed that the leader of each age had a precursor, just as Christ had St. John the Baptist. Even the leader out of the Babylonian captivity, who was to appear in 1260, has such a precursor—in this case, Joachim himself. With the creation of the symbol of the precursor, a new type emerges in Western history: the intellectual who knows the formula for salvation from the misfortunes of the world and can predict how world history will take its course in the future. ... In the further course of Western history, the Christian tide recedes, and the prophet, the precursor of the leader, becomes the secularist intellectual who thinks he knows the meaning of history (understood as world-immanent) and can predict the future.[184]

It is not at all difficult to imagine Dugin viewing himself in precisely such terms.[185] After all, who before Dugin so clearly beheld Russia's significance as the means through which

184   Voegelin, p. 73.
185   "Dugin fully supported this view of the emerging Putin regime [as one fully supporting the Eurasianist ideology] and prophesied that Putin would soon engage in a gothic type of repression against those responsible for the destruction of the USSR. ... Dugin believed he was the one who would provide the regime with intellectual guidance, and it seemed his dreams were about to materialize." (Shlapentokh, p. 35.)

"will be realized the last thought of God, the thought of the End of the World"?

Dugin is the prophet of chaos; as he concludes his book, *The Fourth Political Theory*, he implores his readers to appeal to chaos as to an entity which may be invoked:

> Chaos can think. We should ask her how she does this. We have asked *logos*. Now it is the turn of chaos. We must learn to think with chaos and within the chaos. ...
>
> To make an appeal to chaos is the only way to save *logos*. *Logos* needs a savior, it cannot save itself. ...
>
> In conclusion, it is not correct to conceive chaos as something belonging to the past. Chaos is eternal, but eternally coexisting with time. Therefore, chaos is always absolutely new, fresh, and spontaneous.[186]

Given his adoration of chaos, it is little surprise that the black flag of the Eurasian Movement is adorned with the golden symbol for chaos magic: the eight-pointed star. As Shekhovtsov observed in 2008:

> Occult symbolism plays another important role in Dugin's ideological imagery. The eight-arrow star that became an official symbol of Dugin's organisation had first appeared on the cover of *Osnovy geopolitiki*, posited in the centre of the outline map of Eurasia. Misleadingly identified by Ingram as a swastika, this symbol is a modified 'Star of Chaos' and can be presumed to refer to 'Chaos Magick', an occult doctrine based on the writings of [Aleister] Crowley, Austin Osman Spare and Peter Carroll. ...
>
> The symbolism concerned with the occult teachings of Crowley and the 'Cross Magick' movement constitutes an important element in the style and imagery

of Dugin's doctrine.[187]

Dugin's indulgence in occult symbolism, his seeming-obsession with an end-time struggle between *Arctogaia* and the "Atlantic 'evil empire'"—the Antichrist—paints him in a role more often reserved for prophetic figures, rather than geopoliticians. As Shekhovtsov notes:

> Thus Dugin breaks off with the secular interpretation of the objective reality, and turns his socio-political worldview into a political religion. In its terms, Eurasia is the ultimate 'spiritual' value that – once endangered by a perceived decadent state – must be saved at whatever cost through a 'geopolitical revolution' which would establish the 'New Eurasian Order'. To realise this aim, Dugin's doctrine requires an embodiment in a political regime that would totally subordinate the society to the value(s) of the political religion. This implies that the realisation of the Neo-Eurasian project is only possible under a totalitarian regime.[188]

Eurasianism is thus in keeping with Voegelin's assessment of "gnostic mass movements": "All gnostic movements are involved in the project of abolishing the constitution of being, with its origin in divine, transcendent being, and replacing it with a world-immanent order of being, the perfection of which lies in the realm of human action."[189] The End of the World is the project for which Dugin believes Russia has been appointed, and, if our interpretation is correct, it is to accomplish this end according to the dictates of Eurasian ideology, implemented by the "Supreme Leader" (as Dugin re-

---

187   Anton Shekhovtsov, "The Palingenetic Thrust of Russian Neo-Eurasianism: Ideas of Rebirth in Aleksandr Dugin's Worldview," p. 501.
188   ibid., p. 502.
189   ibid., p. 75.

ferred to him in his January 2001 "Main Principles of Eurasist Policy.")[190]

One final point is worthy of note. Voegelin observed that Joachimite doctrine substitutes the human word (*logos*) for the Divine *Logos* (who is Christ):

> Joachim, too, was dissatisfied with the Augustinian waiting for the end; he, too, wanted to have an intelligible meaning in history here and now; and in order to make the meaning intelligible, he had to set himself up as the prophet to whom this meaning was clear. In the same manner, Hegel identifies his human logos with the Logos that is Christ, in order to make the meaningful process of history fully comprehensible.[191]

For Dugin, *logos* is replaced by chaos, and the very symbol of chaos magic is the symbol of Eurasia: "*Logos* has expired and we all will be buried under its ruins unless we make an appeal to chaos and its metaphysical principles, and use them as a basis for something new."[192] Dugin dressed his discussion of *logos* in the language of Heidegger, but his terminology cannot be read outside of a 2,000 year old Western, biblical tradition which associates the *Logos* with the Christ, and Dugin's invocation of chaos against *logos* leads to certain inevitable conclusions regarding his doctrines.

190   "Main Principles of Eurasist Policy," www.4pt.su.k0.gfns.net/tr/node/30 [Accessed April 18, 2014]
191   Eric Voegelin, *Science, Politics and Gnosticism*, (Wilmington, Delaware: ISI Books, 2004) p. 80.
192   Dugin, *The Fourth Political Theory*, p. 211.

Conclusion

This will be decided by war. The "father of things."[193]

Even as Ukraine was standing on the verge of a vote to elect a new president under the rules of that nation's constitution, as separatist thugs in Donetsk were proclaiming their 'paper republic,' the draft language of the treaty for the Eurasian Economic Union was presented to the governments of Belarus and Kazakstan. As the Belorusian BT news reported on May 15:

> Today Minsk received a draft treaty on the establishment of the Eurasian Economic Union. The document should now pass procedures of intra-state coordination. Initially, it will be considered by national sectoral authorities, on May 20 it will be considered on the meeting of the Council of Ministers.
>
> Yesterday Moscow experts finalized provisions which Presidents of Belarus, Russia and Kazakhstan confirmed at a meeting in Minsk. Thus, the work on the contract is complete. ...
>
> It is expected that a new form of integration will be launched by the presidents of Belarus, Kazakhstan and Russia on May 29 in Astana. And the Eurasian Union will work from January, 1 2015.[194]

Events are proceeding at such a pace that it is difficult to predict what may transpire between the date of publication

---

193   Aleksandr Dugin, "The Hand is Stretching for the Holster…," http://arctogaia.com/public/eng-ed7.htm [Accessed May 15, 2014]

194   http://www.tvr.by/eng/news.asp?id=21007&cid=15 [Accessed May 15, 2014]

of these concluding thoughts, and the beginning of the new year, but several points are worthy of consideration.

First, the Eurasian Union for which Dugin has pined for so many years, and which Putin has promised since October 2011, appears likely to come into existence at the beginning of 2015. This does not mean that it will be (or even become) everything that Dugin has hoped for—but given the number of times that Dugin's Eurasianism has been declared a 'fantasy' from the 'lunatic fringe' by various experts, one should be very circumspect when it comes to trying to guess how far Putin is prepared to go, ultimately, when it comes to realizing the Eurasian Union.

Second, it is becoming clear that an awareness is beginning to grow in the American political culture regarding the geopolitical views of Aleksandr Dugin, and the territorial ambitions of Vladimir Putin and his Eurasian Union. Recent articles for *National Review* by Robert Zubrin, for *Foreign Affairs* by Anton Barbashin and Hannah Thoburn, and for *The New York Review of Books* by Timothy Snyder have all focused attention on Dugin and his ideology. The more the light of public opinion is focused on the threat of Eurasianism, the more likely it is that Western political elites will focus on meeting this rising threat before it can metastasize.

Third, the nations which are slated for initial membership in the Eurasian Union may have grounds to reconsider their own fates as they watch Putin's territorial ambitions play out in Crimea and eastern Ukraine. In a recent article for *The Boston Globe*, Leon Neyfakh noted that the two countries which Putin has thus far convinced to join Russia in forming the Eurasian Union—Belarus and Kazakhstan—"were spooked by Putin's decision to use military force in the situation with Ukraine".[195] In Neyfakh's assessment, Putin may

---

195   Leon Neyfakh, "Putin's long game? Meet the Eurasian Union," *The Boston Globe* (March 9, 2014) www.bostonglobe.com/

have taken the risk of potentially alienating Belarus and Kazakstan precisely because the Eurasian Union is meaningless without Ukraine: "... as the situation in Ukraine continues to unfold, Russia experts have always considered that country the crown jewel—and even a necessary anchor—of any successful version of the Eurasian Union."

It is very important to make Americans aware of the occult nature of Dugin's thought and the way in which his Traditionalist dogma is expressed in his Eurasianist ideology. Dugin has become more circumspect in some of his recent English publications, therefore, it is important to call attention to the overall content and context of his thought.

There is a fundamental demonization of the West which haunts Dugin's thought. This is a necessary aspect of his politicized religious belief. As Mitrofanova wrote concerning the broader phenomena of politicized Orthodoxy in post-Soviet Russia:

> Politicization is understood as a process through which a "normal" religion turns into a religious ideology. The supporters of such ideologies see the world as the arena of confrontation between "us" and "them," but this distinction is not so much between "the Orthodox" and "the non-Orthodox" as between the supporters and the opponents of political Orthodoxy. ... Backers of religion-based ideologies often have no religious faith in the traditional sense; they profess religious ideologies rather than religions.[196]

Again:

> Sacralization of political conflicts entails the demonization of enemies, who become personifications of

---

118

universal Evil. No sacrifices are too extreme and negotiation with the enemy becomes impossible. ... This approach often results in indiscriminate acts of religious terrorism or in suicide terrorist attacks.[197]

One of the clearest examples of such demonization of one's enemies, and of such confrontational "us vs. them" thought which is available in Dugin's English writings is found in an *Elementy* article entitled, "The Hand is Stretching for the Holster...," which is published on his Arctogaia website.[198] The article centers on a notion which Dugin presumes to draw from Heraclitus (535–475 B.C.): "Heraclitus called 'hostility' the 'father of things.'" Dugin thus pontificates on the necessity of aggression as the source of all things: "That is why aggression – is the founding law of existence. Aggression – is the significant and complex, fundamental phenomenon of cosmic reality. In its universality, it may surpass everything else...."[199] Dugin then makes a fundamentally Gnostic dualist claim that "Whatever the type of aggression we would examine, from the very beginning we encounter definitions of two positions, two poles, two borders, between which ripens and bursts a lightning of violence, scorching fire of war." Therefore he breaks down the conflict between "our" (Eurasia) and "not our" ("America and the West"): "Between these poles of 'our' and 'not our' springs up inexorable and terrible hatred. One excludes each other." This aggression, he insists, unifies all the enemies of the West, whatever disagreements might otherwise have divided them in the past:

Anarchists, fascists, communists, left nationalists, nonconformists turn out in the same camp, despite all internal contradictions.

197   Mitrofanova, p. 23.
198   http://arctogaia.com/public/eng-ed7.htm [Accessed May 6, 2014]
199   Note: the ellipsis is in Dugin's original text.

A new map of conflicts and battles, terrorist acts and polemics, attacks and strategic maneuvers is being drawn out. We are entering into a completely unique time of New Aggression, where all former opposites, feuding sides, opponents and enemies are sharply restructuring their ranks. Communists of yesterday are fraternizing with capitalists under the slogans of mondialism, fascists of yesterday are shaking hands with anarchists in diversionary headquarters of the struggle against mondialism.

'Aggression' is not a metaphor for Dugin; he means conflict in the most bloody fashion:

Two positions which could not be brought together, two all-encompassing superworldviews [sic], two mutually exclusive projects of the future of mankind.

Between them is only enmity, hatred, brutal struggle according to rules and without rules, for extermination, to the last drop of blood. Between them are heaps of corpses, millions of lives, endless centuries of suffering and heroic deeds. ...

This will be decided by war. The "father of things."

Reading Dugin's words in "The Hand is Stretching for the Holster...," reminds this writer of the word of warning which an unnamed Sovietologist gave Mark Sedgwick when he traveled to Russia to interview Aleksandr Dugin (and others) in preparation for writing his history of the Traditionalist movement: "Dugin is incredibly erudite, brilliant in his way. ... The main thing to remember is that all these people are 100 percent insane."[200]

---

200   Mark Sedgwick, *Against the Modern World—Traditionalism and the Secret Intellectual History of the Twentieth Century,* (Oxford, New York: Oxford University Press, 2004) p. 3.

Eurasianism is an ideology with two 'faces'—there is its 'geopolitical face' which speaks in terms of a zero-sum competition between international blocs centered on Eurasia and the United States. For those individuals who remember the Cold War, the 'geopolitical face' of Eurasianism is quite familiar because it has a strong family resemblance to the 'geopolitical face' of Marxism–Leninism.

The other 'face' of Eurasianism is the 'occult face'. It is this 'face' which is, at least for Aleksandr Dugin, the more important of the two, and it is the one which, in his ideology, will always constitute the more decisive aspect. An observation which Shenfield made in 2001 continues to provide a crucial insight to Dugin's character: "What has always mattered the most to Dugin is undoubtedly mysticism. It is, after all, with mysticism that Dugin began his intellectual journey as a young initiate of 'the Moscow esoteric elite,' and the mystic remains for him the ultimate reality and the sole source of value."[201]

What Dugin offers the world in Eurasianism is both a geopolitical ideology, and an occult, political religion with its roots in Traditionalist teachings. What remains to be seen is how many adherents of the ideology will also be converted to the religion. However, regardless of the beliefs of particular adherents of Eurasianism, the ultimate ends which Dugin sets forth for Eurasia remain unchanged, a fact which he has driven home in *The Fourth Political Theory*:

> The end times and the eschatological meaning of politics will not realise themselves on their own. We will wait for the end in vain. The end will never come if we wait for it, and it will never come if we do not. This is essential because history, time, and reality have special strategies to avoid Judgment Day, or rather, they have a special strategy of a reversionary manoeuvre that will create the impression that everyone

---

201   Shenfield, p. 198.

has come to a realisation and an understanding. ... If the Fourth Political Practice is not able to realise the end of times, then it would be invalid. The end of days should come; but it will not come by itself. This is a task, it is not a certainty. It is active metaphysics. It is a practice.[202]

When a man says he wants to bring about "the end of days" it certainly does not mean you have to believe that he can do it. But it can be quite informative regarding the man who is making the claim. And Dugin's 'immanentized eschatology' marks Eurasianism to be, above all else, a political religion in the form of a "gnostic mass movement":

Political religions understand the events of this world as a part (or a reflection) of sacral cosmic events. Aims of religiopolitical movements are Aims with a capital "A," vital human endeavors are thought to be sanctioned by supernatural forces. Those who are motivated by political religions do what they do not because they want to do so; instead, they see themselves as following the decree of God or some other supernatural force. It is important to understand that political religions should not be confused with the use of religion for political purposes. Religious politicization implies that political means are used for religious purposes, such as to build God's Kingdom on Earth, an Islamic state, etc. Political power is thereby only the means by which to achieve an ultimately sacral goal.[203]

It is thus that we turn our attention, briefly, to one of the most significant expressions of such political religion which

202   Alexander Dugin, *The Fourth Political Theory,* p. 183.
203   Mitrofanova, p. 22.

122

Dugin offers in the course of his most recent book[204]:

> When there is only one power which decides who is right and who is wrong, and who should be punished and who not, we have a form of global dictatorship. This is not acceptable. Therefore, we should fight against it. If someone deprives us of our freedom, we have to react. And we will react. The American Empire should be destroyed. And at one point, it will be.
>
> Ideologically, unipolarity is based on modernist and postmodernist values that are openly anti-traditional ones. I share the vision of René Guénon and Julius Evola, who considered modernity and its ideological basis (individualism, liberal democracy, capitalism, consumerism, and so on) to be the cause of the future catastrophe of humanity, and the global domination of the Western lifestyle as the reason for the final degradation of the Earth. The West is approaching its terminus, and we should not let it drag all the rest of us down into the abyss with it.
>
> Spiritually, globalisation is the creation of a grand parody, the kingdom of the Antichrist. And the United States is the centre of its expansion. American values pretend to be 'universal' ones. In reality, it is a new form of ideological aggression against the multiplicity of cultures and traditions still existing in the rest of the world.[205]

At the beginning of the passage, Dugin appears to be simply making a geopolitical assertion like those which he has made

---

204   *The Fourth Political Theory* deserves a more detailed examination than it can be granted here; no doubt the current writer will need to consider returning to that task in the near future.

205   Alexander Dugin, *The Fourth Political Theory*, p. 193.

over and over again. It appears—at first—to be an assertion that a unipolar world (i.e., one dominated by Western civilization) would be bad, while a multipolar world would be good. The references to the "American Empire," "the West," and the "United States" allow for a geopolitical interpretation of the passage.

But when Dugin declares that "globalisation is ... the kingdom of the Antichrist. And the United States is the centre of its expansion," one begins to realize that what is being made is a theological, rather than a strictly geopolitical, observation. The corpus of Dugin's demon-haunted prose is filled with too many apocalyptic references to incline one to read such a reference to "the kingdom of the Antichrist" as some sort of hyperbole.

Western interpreters of Dugin have often been shocked by the occult character of his view of the world. As Allensworth observed:

> If one is Orthodox, then one believes Orthodoxy to be the Truth. How can Dugin reconcile that with his practically universalistic views? In Dugin's philosophy, Orthodoxy is "only one of many possible paths to the realization of Tradition." ... That is to say nothing of Dugin's fascination with the occult (including Satanism) and the postmodern quality of Dugin's eclectic philosophy, including European geopolitics and strategy, Gnostic mysticism, occultism, "traditionalism," and his advocacy of "leftist fascism and rightist communism."[206]

It would be our argument, then, that Dugin's assertion— "When there is only one power which decides who is right and who is wrong, and who should be punished and who not, we have a form of global dictatorship"—should be read first

206   Allensworth, p. 116.

as a theological assertion, and only after that as a geopolitical one. If this is an accurate assessment, Dugin's first complaint is that there is an assertion of one Truth—against the panoply of Traditions—to be found opposing his "practically universalistic" views. The audacity of the United States—a place where Protestants and Roman Catholics culturally predominate and yet live in peace—to imagine *they* know the Truth enrages Dugin. (After all, from his perspective, such Americans are utterly lacking a valid 'Tradition'!) To this writer, it seems as if there is a rage behind such passages in Dugin's writings which rebels at the notion that there is One Who Decides, and Who Judges. If this is accurate, then it is His decrees that lead Dugin to rage against His "global dictatorship" and to call upon his readers to invoke chaos, and abandon *logos*.

But we are *not* as those upon "a darkling plain/Swept with confused alarms of struggle and flight/where ignorant armies clash by night."[207] And the reality which confronts the West is not, ultimately, some profound mystery uncovered by a mystic who has stepped forth from the pages of a Dostoyevsky novel, any more than the West confronted some profound and invincible economic law when it stopped the forces of Marxism-Leninism from turning the world into a vast prison camp. Eurasianism—viewed from the standpoint of citizens of the American Republic—is an attempt to excuse the efforts by one nation to enslave other nations in the name of some otherworldly purpose. Despite the pomposity of Eurasianist rhetoric, there is no need, no necessity, for the black flag of Eurasianism to flutter over nations which have been enslaved anew.

Victory requires commitment, but victory is most certainly attainable. As Peter Schweizer observed twenty years ago in his book, *Victory*:

> The Soviet Union did not collapse by osmosis, nor because time was somehow on our side. Had the

---

207   From "Dover Beach" (1867) by Matthew Arnold.

Kremlin not faced the cumulative effects of SDI and the defense buildup, geopolitical setbacks in Poland and Afghanistan, the loss of tens of billions of dollars in hard currency earnings from energy exports, and reduced access to technology, it is reasonable to believe that it could have weathered the storm. Soviet communism was not an organism doomed to self-destruct in any international environment. American policies could and did alter the course of Soviet history.[208]

The incipient Eurasian Union is a far cry from the force which was the Soviet Union, and it is no more invincible nor eternal than the denizens of the Kremlin imagined their last ideology would be. The blood of the martyrs of Kiev calls out. Let us hear their voices before they are joined by the ranks of a new *Holodomor*.

In 1970, Aleksandr Solzhenitsyn received the Nobel Prize "for the ethical force with which he has pursued the indispensable traditions of Russian literature."[209] In his *Nobel Lecture*, Solzhenitsyn observed:

But let us not forget that violence does not and cannot exist by itself: It is invariably intertwined with *the lie*. They are linked in the most intimate, most organic and profound fashion: Violence cannot conceal itself behind anything except lies, and lies have nothing to maintain them save violence. Anyone who has once proclaimed violence as his *method* must inexorably choose the lie as his *principle*.[210]

208   Peter Schweizer, *Victory—The Reagan Administration's Secret Strategy that Hastened the Collapse of the Soviet Union*, (New York: The Atlantic Monthly Press, 1994) p. 282.
209   The text of Solzhenitsyn's *Nobel Lecture* is contained in *The Solzhenitsyn Reader—New and Essential Writings, 1947–2005*, ed. by Edward E. Ericson, Jr. and Daniel J. Mahoney, (Wilmington, Deleware; ISI Books, 2006) p. 513–526.
210   ibid., p. 526.

Eurasianism has chosen violence as its method, even as its chief proponent speaks of "sacred geography" and the battle of Hyperborea against the West. In the face of Eurasianists who seek to exceed the imperial grasp of the U.S.S.R., we reply with the words of Solzhenitsyn:

> The simple act of an ordinary brave man is not to participate in lies, not to support false actions! His rule: Let *that* come into the world, let it even reign supreme—only not through me. ...
> The favorite proverbs in Russian are about *truth*. They forcefully express a long and difficult national experience, sometimes in striking fashion:
> *One word of truth shall outweigh the whole world.*[211]

The West has been built upon the foundations of Athens and Jerusalem—the history of the West has been one of a quest to seek and uphold the truth. The answer to a postmodern disinterest in truth is not to substitute a lie in place of the truth, or to invoke chaos while abandoning *Logos*, but to return to the truth.

---

211   ibid.

JAMES D. HEISER, is the Bishop of the Evangelical Lutheran Diocese of North America (ELDoNA) and Pastor of Salem Lutheran Church (Malone, Texas). He also serves as Dean of Missions for The Augustana Ministerium and as a member both of the Board of Directors and Steering Committee of The Mars Society.

Heiser earned his B.A.–Political Science at George Washington University (Washington, D.C.) and his M.Div. and S.T.M. from Concordia Theological Seminary (Fort Wayne, Indiana).

Heiser is the author of six books: one recounting the course of the Hermetic Reformation (*Prisci Theologi and the Hermetic Reformation in the Fifteenth Century*), a collection of essays concerning the Office of the Holy Ministry (*Stewards of the Mysteries of God*), two books of essays pertaining to space exploration and theology (*A Shining City on a Higher Hill* and *Civilization and the New Frontier*) and two books on the crises of the Modern age (*A Time for Every Purpose Under Heaven* and *The One True God, the Two Estates and the Three Kingdoms*). He is also the author of hundreds of published articles.

Made in the USA
Las Vegas, NV
22 March 2022

46112275R00075